TRACING YOUR GREAT WAR ANCESTORS

Ypres

FAMILY HISTORY FROM PEN & SWORD

TRACING YOUR GREAT WAR ANCESTORS

Ypres

A Guide for Family Historians

Simon Fowler

Pen & Sword
FAMILY HISTORY

First published in Great Britain in 2015
PEN & SWORD FAMILY HISTORY
an imprint of
Pen & Sword Books Ltd
47 Church Street
Barnsley
South Yorkshire
S70 2AS

ISBN 978 1 47382 370 9

A CIP catalogue record for this book is
available from the British Library.

Typeset in Palatino and Optima by
CHIC GRAPHICS

Printed and bound in England by
CPI Group (UK), Croydon, CR0 4YY

Pen & Sword Books Ltd incorporates the imprints of Pen & Sword
Archaeology, Atlas, Aviation, Battleground, Discovery, Family History,
History, Maritime, Military, Naval, Politics, Railways, Select, Social History,
Transport, True Crime, Claymore Press, Frontline Books, Leo Cooper,
Praetorian Press, Remember When, Seaforth Publishing and Wharncliffe.

For a complete list of Pen & Sword titles please contact
PEN & SWORD BOOKS LTD
47 Church Street, Barnsley, South Yorkshire, S70 2AS, England
E-mail: enquiries@pen-and-sword.co.uk
Website: www.pen-and-sword.co.uk

CONTENTS

LIST OF ABBREVIATIONS

Army paperwork is full of abbreviations which can be puzzling to the novice, and the following list provides definitions for the most common ones.

ACI	Army Council Instruction
ADS	Advanced Dressing Station
AIF	Australian Imperial Force
ASC	Army Service Corps
BEF	British Expeditionary Force
BRCS	British Red Cross Society
BWM	British War Medal
CEF	Canadian Expeditionary Force
CCS	Casualty Clearing Station
CLC	Chinese Labour Corps
CO	Commanding officer
Cpl	Corporal
Cpt	Captain
CQMS	Company Quartermaster Sergeant
CRA	Commanding Royal Artillery
CRE	Commanding Royal Engineers
CSM	Company Sergeant Major
FP	Field Punishment
GCM	General Court Martial
GHQ	General Headquarters
GOC	General Officer Commanding
GSW	Gunshot Wound
HA	Heavy Artillery
HE	Heavy Explosive
HS	Home Service

HAC	Honourable Artillery Company
IOR	Indian Other Rank
KIA	Killed in Action
KR	King's Regulations
KRRC	King's Royal Rifle Corps
L/Cpl	Lance Corporal
LofC	Lines of Communication
L/Sgt	Lance Sergeant
Lt	Lieutenant
Lt Col	Lieutenant Colonel
MGC	Machine Gun Corps
MiD	Mentioned in Despatches
NCO	Non-commissioned Officer
OC	Officer Commanding
OR	Other Rank(s)
POW	Prisoner of War
Pte	Private
PU	Permanently Unfit (found in service records)
QAIMNS	Queen Alexandra's Imperial Military Nursing Service
QARNNC	Queen Alexandra's Royal Naval Nursing Corps
RA	Royal Artillery
RAF	Royal Air Force
RAMC	Royal Army Medical Corps
RE	Royal Engineers
RFC	Royal Flying Corps
RFA	Royal Field Artillery
RGA	Royal Garrison Artillery
RHA	Royal Horse Artillery
RNAS	Royal Naval Air Service
RND	Royal Naval Division
SAA	Small Arms Ammunition
Sgt	Sergeant
TF	Territorial Force

VAD   Voluntary Aid Detachment
WAAC   Women's Army Auxiliary Corps
WO   War Office

The Long, Long Trail provides a comprehensive list of abbreviations at www.1914-1918.net/abbrev.htm.

INTRODUCTION

Even after a century the First World War and, in particular, the Western Front exerts a powerful attraction on millions of people. To us the war seems senseless, which makes it even more of a tragedy. But nowhere was it a greater tragedy than along the Western Front in Belgium. Hundreds of thousands of young men lost their lives or suffered life-shortening wounds in the mud of Flanders, in the 'Immortal Salient', in the words of one contemporary writer. The local Flemish people saw their livelihoods and their houses destroyed before they were forced out of the war zone altogether. But there were many heroic actions – recorded and unrecorded – and many men felt their time in the Army was one of the highlights of their life.

This short book attempts to offer a guide to researching the men and units who fought in Belgium. With so much material now online it is fairly easy to do, although there are a number of shell holes to trap the unwary and so keep things interesting. However, there is very little here about the fighting itself – there are dozens of books that explain, in a far better way than I ever could, what went on in greater or lesser detail – instead I have tried to give a glimpse of what it was like to be in the Salient during the war. There is also a section devoted to visiting the battlefields today (and what it was like visiting ninety years ago), because you should go if you have not already done so.

My personal links to the battlefields are not strong. My Great-Uncle Rifleman 44005 Stanley Crozier, 18th King's Royal Rifle Corps certainly spent time in Flanders during 1918. Unfortunately, he was killed three weeks before the Armistice by a stray shell when his unit was bivouacked outside a village near Kortrijk (Courtrai) during the Final Push to victory. And I have been on a number of trips to the Salient since the mid-1980s, when visitors to the battlefields were still fairly rare, up to the present day when battlefield tourism is now big business and likely to grow further between now and 2018.

There is a danger that the First World War has become sanitised to meet the needs of a more squeamish sentimental generation, think of the emphasis on the Christmas Truce, horses and the fallacy that Britain need not have gone to war in August 1914. The Great War was brutal, bloody and broke many a good man. And it was undoubtedly made worse by a high command slow to learn the lessons of trench warfare and total war, although critics at the time, and subsequently, have failed to come up with any satisfactory alternatives.

The sideshows in Italy, Salonika, Palestine and, above all, Gallipoli were just that, sideshows draining men and materiel for little real contribution to ultimate victory over the Central Powers of Germany, Austria-Hungary, Bulgaria and Turkey. It was clear that ultimate victory had to come on the Western Front – the 450 miles of trenches, barbed wire and decomposing bodies which began in the boggy marshes around Nieuwport on the North Sea coast and snaked around Ypres and thence through Northern France and the Vosges mountains to reach Switzerland at the small border crossing at Pfefferhausen.

The Revd Tubby Clayton, who had spent much of the War at Poperinge, crossed the Western Front on 10 November to the newly liberated areas to the east. He found:

On each side there is a crescendo of desolation. Trees first scarred, then blasted, then stumps, then non-existent. Houses first roofless, then barely recognisable, then pieces of wall with dugouts against or under them, then brick-heaps; then vanished utterly. If you dug you might find bricks, even floors and cellars; but it is wiser not to. For the rest, wire all rusted and tangled, rotting sandbags, broken

wheels, piles of unused shells, boxes of ammunition, timber
for the roads, duckboard tracks, grotesque direction posts
in two languages, dead mules flung into inadequate shell
holes go on in one vast nightmare across the rise and fall
of the ground . . .

The aims were simple: either the Germans would drive the
British into the sea and take Paris, or the British, French and their
allies would push the Germans back towards the Rhine. Whoever
succeeded would be the winner.

At the simplest the winner would be the country which
produced the most shells and who killed more of the enemy.
Passchendaele (Third Ypres) in particular was a breathtakingly
horrifying plan to bleed the German Army dry: that is to kill more
of their men than they managed to kill of ours. And although the
figures have been disputed, it is clear that, in this respect at least,
the plan worked. In the Official History, Brigadier-General J. E.
Edmonds put British casualties at 244,897 and claimed that
estimated German losses were around 400,000 men. After the war
the German General Staff concluded: 'Germany had been
brought near to certain destruction by the Flanders battle of
1917.'

To secure this victory the economies of Britain, France and
Germany were transformed. Millions of men joined the forces
and women entered the labour market in unprecedented
numbers, taking over from their menfolk who had enlisted or
working in huge new factories making munitions, aircraft or
tanks. And a small number even enlisted and saw service on the
Western Front, although none were close to the fighting.
Meanwhile, every aspect of the citizen's life at home was being
regulated as never before: what they ate, how they occupied their
leisure hours, and even when they visited the pub.

For over three years from October and November 1914 when
the opposing armies ground to a halt along what both sides called

the Western Front there was stalemate, because neither side was strong enough to defeat the other. Millions of shells and bullets were fired and hundreds of thousands of men were killed or mutilated in futile attempts to break this deadlock. Cunningly, the Germans generally occupied the high ground, which made it that much more difficult for British and French attacks to succeed. Thereafter, the Germans strengthened their positions and repelled attack after attack.

The old certainties were broken in March 1918 when Germans suddenly swept aside British and French forces advancing deep into France. Operation Michael was a gamble that almost worked but within weeks ground to a halt because the advancing troops could not easily be resupplied. Around Ypres too the Germans made small gains and forced civilians and non-essential troops to flee from Popringe.

In turn the 'Hundred Days' of the Allied advance began in August. Military historians have called it the greatest British military triumph of all, although in all honesty it was against an increasingly enfeebled and demoralised enemy. At Ypres the British only began to advance at the end of September. The Germans finally agreed to an Armistice on St Martin's Day, 11 November 1918. They had had little choice because the stresses of the war had finally caused a revolution back home (and increasingly there was unrest in the Army as well).

As is well known, in 1914 the British Expeditionary Force (BEF) was tiny in comparison with European armies, but it was well-trained and well-led, so accounted for itself very well in the first bloody encounters with the Germans. And bloody they were: by the end of 1914 the BEF had received 90 per cent casualties, that is, nine out of ten men were either killed or wounded to some degree. In many ways these battles were more akin to those fought in the Napoleonic Wars to any fought subsequently. According to Max Hastings:

Contrary to the popular myth that 1 July 1916, the first day of the Somme, was the bloodiest day of the conflict, in reality this was 22 August 1914, when France lost 27,000 [men]. The British army fought its first battle at Mons the following day, then, on 26 August at Le Cateau, they staged a rearguard action that is almost forgotten today, but that resulted in roughly the same losses as D-day in Normandy, 1944.

After the Western Front settled down the British were assigned the area around Ypres to defend. It was where the British had arrived in October 1914, at one of the last places where trenches had yet to be built. With great sacrifice they stopped the advancing Germans.

The Western Front took a detour around the town: it was less than an hour's brisk march from Ypres to the front line. The Western Front then went south around the small villages of Ploegstreet (Plug Street to the British) and Menen (Menin) to the French border near Armentières. These were generally much quieter areas.

To the north were the Belgians, who occupied the line through the marshy lowlands north from Dixmude to the North Sea coast, and from Armentières to the south lay the French. As British reinforcements grew during 1915 the French handed over the area of the Western Front north of the Somme River. And for periods in September and October 1914 and the summer of 1918 there were also British troops on the Marne, the part of the Western Front closest to Paris.

Apart for a few hours on 14 October 1914 Ypres remained in British hands throughout the war. It lay in a salient jutting into German lines that surrounded the town on three sides. The town possessed a strategic importance far great that its size warranted. There are several reasons for this:

An aerial photograph of Ypres taken in 1919 showing a little of the devastation suffered by the town. (Author)

- It protected the Channel seaports of Dunkirk, Boulogne and Calais from German attack. And without these ports it would have been almost impossible to reinforce British forces along the rest of the Western Front. In turn Ypres offered a good position from which to advance to seize Ostend, so preventing the Germans using the port for U-boat attacks on Allied shipping. Taking Ostend was one of the objectives of the Battle of Passchendaele;
- Psychologically, defending Ypres was very important to the Belgian people as it represented the last part of Belgium land still under its sovereignty;

- Because of the gallant bravery displayed in saving the town from the Germans in 1914, against overwhelming odds, the town became a symbol of defiance. To have been driven out of Ypres would have been a catastrophic blow to British morale. One of the veterans, Captain Hugh Pollard, writing in the *Pilgrim's Guide to the Ypres Salient*, published in 1919, said that the town: 'stood as a synonym of sacrifice, bitter endurance and suffering, ultimately crowned by the laurels of victory'.

To understand how the war was fought in the Salient it is necessary to understand the terrain around Ypres. From the air the town appears to be at the centre of a shallow basin. Both to the east and to the west are low, partly wooded hills, with some small hamlets and farms. You hardly notice them as you drive through the area by car or even on a bicycle. The highest point of the Messines Ridge, for example, is no more than 264ft (80m) above sea level.

When the front lines had stabilised in November 1914, the Germans were in command of the ridges to the east of Ypres. This was a deliberate decision on their part. They were helped by the fact that during the Second Battle of Ypres in April and May 1915 they captured what remaining high ground lay in British hands. This gave a massive strategic advantage, as it is much easier to defend high ground. The Third Battle of Ypres in the summer and autumn of 1915, for example, was largely a painfully slow slog up a long slope by the British to the village of Passchendaele, made worse because the Germans were so well dug-in at the top of the ridge. And in possessing the heights the Germans could easily observe and attempt to disrupt Allied preparations all around Ypres, which they did on a daily basis.

The flat low-lying area around Ypres itself was criss-crossed by streams and dykes draining into the canalised River Yser, which flows north–west towards the North Sea. The military historian Paddy Griffith succinctly described the area in his *Battle Tactics of*

A deep shell hole near the Yser Canal showing a little of the mud so closely associated with the Ypres Salient. (Author)

the Western Front (1994) as being 'an evil waterlogged and overlooked spot'.

The 1920 Michelin Guide to the battlefields around Ypres noted that:

the war [here] assumed a character entirely different from the rest of the front. The marshy ground almost at sea level is further sodden by constant rain and mists and forms a spongy mass, in which it was impossible to dig trenches and underground shelters. Water is found immediately below the surface so that the only possible defence works were parapets. The bursting shell holes made huge craters which, promptly filling with water, became so many death-traps for wounded and unwounded alike.

So any point more than a few metres above sea level became an important defensive point. The 1920 Michelin Guide continues: 'The defence on both sides consequently centred around the woods, villages and numerous farms, which were converted into redoubts with concrete blockhouses and deep wire entanglements. The slightest bits of rising ground here played an important part and were fiercely disputed.' And a guide to the German defences around Ypres from the 1930s was envious that:

The British attacks . . . were delivered from shell holes, from water-logged and demolished trenches, over ground which in many cases nothing less than a veritable quagmire, against perfectly sited and admirably constructed defences manned by soldiers whose fighting quality has never been in doubt . . .

On the British side some idea seems to have been current that such works were not worth the labour or the cost, but probably the real reason was the fear that a lack of offensive spirit might have been engendered if the troops had been provided with such defences.

This led to the muddy hell that was the Battle of Passchendaele. Paddy Griffith suggests the very word Passchendaele has 'a particularly liquid resonance about it, reminding us that many of the wounded were destined to drown where they lay and many of the tactical movements sank literally waist deep in the mud'. Before the war Iper (the Flemish name for Ypres) was a market town and provincial centre. In medieval times it had been a prosperous wool town. The imposing Cloth Hall – the Lakenhalle in Dutch – on the main square and St Martin's Cathedral behind it are reminders of this. In 1914, Ypres, which the Michelin Guide described as being a 'clean well-built town', had a population of 18,000 largely engaged in the manufacture of linen, cotton goods and lace. There was also a modest tourist trade. The Cloth Hall in particular drew visitors. In his travel book *One Day's Tour*, published in 1887, Percy Hetherington Fitzgerald thought it was 'astonishing'. He said that it 'was the largest, most massive, solid and enduring thing that can be conceived'. But he found the town itself curiously deserted: 'One might have starved or famished without relief. Nay, there was hardly a public house or drinking shop.'

During the first few months of the war Ypres was hardly touched, although many citizens became refugees in France. The destruction of the town really took place in April and May 1915, as part of what became known as the Second Battle of Ypres.

Brigadier Morgan Crofton marched with his troops through the town on 21 May 1915. He had previously been there in February, but now found:

> Having passed the end of the Cloth Hall we turned to our left, and gained the square. Our engineers had been busy most of the day burning any house which might impede the aim of our guns; as we passed the corner house, a fire, which had been for some time internally combusting in the cellar, burst out and engulfed with a roar the whole structure in its inflammatory embrace. By the light of this house we wended our way across the square.
>
> Here the change from our previous visit was even more marked. The burnt out shells of houses, roofless and windowless, surrounded the square, houses which before had been full of buyers and sellers, and doing good trade. The smell of dead horses was disgusting. Dotted about the square were heaps of these unfortunate animals each

smouldering and pointing to the abortive attempts of scavengers to clear up by burning. A few wrecked waggons added to the gaiety of the scene. As we crossed the Eastern end of the square, a few random shrapnel came with a whine and a shriek over our heads and burst in the battered and mutilated Cloth Hall.

The civilian population was now forcibly removed from the town and only returned after the Armistice.

The small town of Poperinge lay 8 miles (13km) to the west in the very rural area known as the Westhoek. This was all that

The ruined Cloth Hall and Grand Place, Ypres. The Cloth Hall in particular became a symbol of the Allied determination not to let the town fall to the Germans. (Author)

remained of unoccupied Belgium: the rest lay under increasingly brutal German control. The area around Poperinge was slowly transformed into one great British military base with hospitals, rest areas, training bases, ammunition dumps, repair shops and the like. The Revd Tubby Clayton, who ran Talbot House, a social club for soldiers, in the town, noted that Poperinge 'was without a rival locally . . . close enough to the line to be directly accessible to the principal sufferers, and not so near as to be positively ruinous, it became metropolitan not by merit but by the logic of locality'. In November 1915 he marvelled, that 'This afternoon – think of it – we are all going to the cinema to tea and "movies". And this with the Germans thundering away on three sides of us. What a world of contrasts it all is!'

Now almost the only reminder of this occupation are the

A postcard of Poperinge showing British troops in 1914 or early 1915. (Wikipedia)

Commonwealth War Graves Commission cemeteries located where the hospitals and casualty clearing stations once where.

Poperinge combined being a centre of military activity with a place for the troops to relax and escape the war, with dozens of bars and restaurants. Here could be found men from a dozen different nationalities. Soldiers from the British Isles, Canada, Australia and New Zealand, from India, Portugal, America, Belgium, France and the French colonies, and labourers from the British West Indies and China, together with German prisoners of war. They rubbed shoulders with the locals, who served in shops, ran the estaminets and continued to till the land almost up to the front as best they could. Tubby Clayton said that: 'The shops open up gaily among the battered houses and sell anything they can, mainly beer which is the colour and consistency of bathwater, and floral postcards of coloured silk in which the soul of Tommy takes high delight.' Tubby's creation, Talbot House, still operates in the town.

THE WESTERN FRONT ASSOCIATION

If you become passionate about the First World War you should consider joining the Western Front Association. The Association exists to further interest in the Great War of 1914–18 and aims to perpetuate the memory, courage and comradeship of all those on all sides who served their countries in France and Flanders. Members are a mixture of academics, enthusiasts and family historians. The Association publishes four journals and four comprehensive newsletters a year, organises several conferences and now runs an excellent and informative website at www.westernfrontassociation.com. At the time of writing membership is £26 per annum.

Chapter 1

GETTING STARTED

This chapter offers basic guidance whether you are interested in researching soldiers or the units they served in and around Ypres.

Online Resources

There are four major data providers with significant First World War content online: Ancestry, Findmypast, the Naval and Military Archive and The National Archives. Which one you choose depends on what you are looking for, which may of course include records that do not necessarily relate to the First World War.

Ancestry (www.ancestry.co.uk) is undoubtedly the best place to start. It is a subscription site: you pay for a year's unlimited access to the data. If you are not already a subscriber it is worth trying the free fourteen-day trial. Alternatively access is free at many local libraries. However, it is of little use if your interest is primarily not genealogical. With the exception of the Medal Index Cards, much the same material is available on Findmypast (www.findmypast.co.uk), although they also have one or two unique resources of their own, notably access to hundreds of historic newspapers.

If your interest is solely First World War then you might consider the Naval and Military Archive (www.nmarchive.com) from Naval & Military Press. You can subscribe for a day, week, month or year. The main resources here are Unit War Diaries and transcripts of Campaign Medal Rolls, including the Silver War

Badge. There are a few smaller databases as well, which also can be found on Ancestry and Findmypast. Although extremely useful, it is perhaps not aimed at the total beginner. In addition, most of the resources can be found on other sites.

The National Archives provides online access to service records for men who served in the Royal Navy and the Royal Air Force and the few women who joined the services during the war. You can also download war diaries, Cabinet papers (if you are interested in the strategic and diplomatic side of the war) and air combat reports. Some material is free, such as the Cabinet papers, but in general you pay to download specific documents, which come as PDFs. At time of writing this was £3.30 per document. A document might just be a single-page service record or hundreds of pages of a war diary.

There is also the Forces War Records. It is hard to know exactly what they have available for the First World War, but it is unlikely they have any of the key databases. More useful may be The Genealogist, which uniquely has the War Office Weekly Casualty Lists as well as the Distinguished Conduct Medal and Military Medal cards, together with various other minor datasets that can be found elsewhere. It is a subscription site. Details at www.thegenealogist.co.uk.

Not everything is online by any means. Particularly if you decide to do an in-depth study of an individual or research a particular unit or action you are likely to need to use original papers, letters and files that are probably to be found in an archive. If you want to know more about what archives are and how to use them there are a series of Quick Animated Guides at www.nationalarchives. gov.uk/records/quick-animated-guides.htm.

There are three major types of archives with some overlap between their holdings. The most important is The National Archives (TNA) in Kew which has almost all the surviving service and operational records for the three services plus much else besides. In this book assume that the records described are held by The National Archives (TNA) unless indicated otherwise. TNA has an excellent website – www.nationalarchives.gov.uk – which will help you find the records you are looking for and prepare for a visit. In particular, Research Signposts, and the more detailed Research Guides, explain the records very simply. Find them at www.nationalarchives.gov.uk/records.

The records themselves are described via the Discovery catalogue. The catalogue describes all 11 million documents available for researchers at Kew. The descriptions are often pretty general, but should be good enough for you to work out which are likely to be useful to you. However, an increasing number of documents are available indexed by individual, such as all the service men and women (as well as a few civilians) who appear in the Medal Index Cards.

Regimental and service museums and archives have records relating to their service or regiment. The big service museums are the Imperial War Museum (for all services), the National Army Museum and the RAF Museum. Addresses are given below. In addition there is the Royal Naval Museum in Portsmouth, although there is little here about the Western Front.

The National Army Museum also has some papers from the Irish regiments disbanded in 1922 (that is the Royal Dublin and Royal Munster Fusiliers, Connaught Rangers, Royal Leinster and Royal Irish regiments and the South Irish Horse), the Indian Army (whose records are shared with the British Library), Middlesex Regiment and the East Kent Regiment (The Buffs). However, the Museum is closed for rebuilding until 2016 and access to their archives are rather limited as a result.

In addition, most regiments have their own regimental museum and archive, although their archives are increasingly likely to be found at the appropriate county record office. These archives may include collections of regimental orders, personal papers and photographs, war diaries (which may duplicate those at Kew), regimental magazines, registers and records which TNA for one reason or another did not want. Each of these archives has very different collections, so you may strike lucky or go away almost empty-handed. Most welcome visitors, but you usually have to make an appointment. The Army Museums Ogilby Trust maintains a very good website which links to museum websites and provides details about individual regimental museums at www.armymuseums.org.uk.

Service and regimental museums DO NOT have any service records: these are either at TNA or, for men who left after the end of 1920, with the Ministry of Defence.

County archives (or record offices) may have relevant material, particularly relating to the impact of the war on local communities. A few have the regimental archives deposited by the local regiment: the Durham County Record Office, for example, has records of the Durham Light Infantry. There may also be records of Territorial Force battalions, rolls of honour and files about war memorials.

There are also many more specialist repositories ranging from the British Library, which is comparable to TNA in size and importance, to company and hospital archives. With the exception of the British Library, which has records of the Indian Army, they are not likely to hold much direct information about the war.

To find the addresses, websites and other contact details of all British (and some overseas) archives visit ARCHON – www.nationalarchives.gov.uk/archon – where there are links to the websites of individual archives. For regimental museums, however, it may be easier to go via www.armymuseums.org.uk.

In addition, there are two national databases showing which records are held where. The National Register of Archives (www.nationalarchives.gov.uk/nra) offers broad descriptions of particular collections of records held at archives across the United Kingdom – this is particularly useful if you are looking to see whether there are papers for an individual or company. Access to Archives (www.nationalarchives.gov.uk/a2a) offers more

British soldiers walking through the ruined village of Wijsheate during the Battle of Messines. (Author)

detailed descriptions of the holdings of many archives in England. You might want to use this to search for generic references to Ypres or Passchendaele, rather than for the records of an individual. The data from these websites has recently been added to TNA's Discovery Catalogue and it may be easier to use this than the separate databases. There is also an equivalent for Wales (www.archivesnetworkwales.info) and in Scotland the Scottish Archive Network provides something similar at www.scan.org.uk.

Using online catalogues can be tricky, particularly those provided by local record offices, so if there are any instructions it is a good idea to read them before you start. In general, the more information you type in the more it will confuse the search engine, so try to keep it simple.

Useful Addresses

British Library, 96 Euston Road, London NW1 2DB; www.bl.uk

Imperial War Museum, Lambeth Road, London SE1 6HZ; www.iwm.org.uk

The National Archives, Ruskin Avenue, Kew, Richmond TW9 4DU; www.nationalarchives.gov.uk

National Army Museum, Royal Hospital Road, London SW3 4HT; www.national-army-museum.org.uk; the Museum is closed until 2016 for rebuilding and until that time there is only limited access to their archival collections

RAF Museum, Graeme Park Way, London NW9 5LL; www.rafmuseum.org.uk

Royal Naval Museum, HM Naval Base, Portsmouth PO1 3NH; www.royalnavalmuseum.org/research.htm

Army Museums Ogilby Trust; www.armymuseums.org.uk

Chapter 2

RESEARCHING SOLDIERS

In this chapter we look at the basic records you can use to get a general picture of an ancestor's service.

Nearly 6 million men (and 50,000 women) served in the British Army during the First World War – many of whom saw service in Flanders – and, although some records are missing, you should be able to find something about each of them. However, exactly what cannot be predicted with any certainty. What survives varies enormously, which is one of the great charms of researching the First World War, although it can be frustrating if you find there is very little about your man.

But before you start you need to be reasonably confident of the soldier's full name, the regiment or other unit he served with, and – ideally – his service number (that is if he was an ordinary soldier or non-commissioned officer). Otherwise it is very easy to start researching the wrong person.

It is important to remember all the possible variations of a man's name. I recently researched a Douglas Tyler of the 10th Sherwood Foresters, who was posted as being Missing in Action on 14 December 1915. There is a memorial to him – as Douglas Tyler – at Mackworth churchyard, but on the Menin Gate Memorial to the Missing he is down as A. D. Tyler. And his Medal Index Card calls him Albert Tyler. We know he is the same man because his regimental number is the same.

If you have a soldier's medals the information should stamped on the rim or back. Or it may appear on any family papers such as letters and diaries or even written on the back of photographs.

Family stories can also help, although often only general statements such as, 'he was at Passchendaele' or 'he was in the trenches when he was buried by an explosion' are not very useful. Even so they may offer a clue.

Each man's records are different and you never know what you are going to find. In general, however, there is likely to be more information for men who enlisted early in the war, saw front-line service or who were killed in action.

Medal Index Cards

Every serviceman and woman (as well as a few civilians) who saw service overseas was entitled to two campaign medals, the British War Medal and the Victory Medal. In addition, men who had seen service in France and Flanders between 5 August and midnight of 22/23 November 1914 were awarded the 1914 Star (sometimes erroneously called the Mons Star) and men who served overseas between 5 August 1914 and 31 December 1915 were entitled to the 1914/15 Star. Occasionally, you may find a reference to the Territorial Force War Medal which was awarded to men who were members of the Territorial Forces at the beginning of the war and later who saw service overseas, but were not eligible for the 1914 or 1914/15 Stars. My Great-Uncle Stanley Crozier was one such recipient – his territorial unit served in India until 1916, when he managed to get a posting to 'France and Flanders'. Each medal was stamped with the man's name and rank and number current at the time of his discharge.

Details of individual recipients are to be found on Medal Rolls and on Medal Index Cards. If you can't find a man's name here then you can assume that for one reason or another he did not leave the British Isles.

There are several designs of Medal Index Card, but regardless of which design you come across they should tell you: the rank he held at the end of his service; regimental numbers (other ranks

The Medal Index Card for James Harold Wheatley gives brief details of his Army career as well as the campaign medals he was entitled to. (Ancestry/The National Archives)

only); the units he served in; the medals to which he was entitled together with the page on the Medal Roll where details are to be found; the date he went overseas (if this was before the end of 1915); and the theatre of war in which he served – the Western Front was shown as being F&F for 'France and Flanders' or the number 1 or 1A.

In addition, there may be further information such as: the date of discharge or when he was killed in action (KIA) or died of wounds (DofW); the gallantry medals a man was awarded, something to that he was entitled to wear the oak leaf emblem on the Victory Medal for being Mentioned in Despatches, usually abbreviated to EMB; a note he was entitled to wear a clasp (actually a silver rose) on his 1914 Star, which indicates that he had served within the sound of enemy guns, usually indicated by the word 'clasp'; and whether he was discharged to the Z Reserve in 1919, that is he could be recalled in the event of resumption of hostilities with Germany. There may also be heavy abbreviated notes about correspondence with the medal holder or his family generally about what medals the individual was entitled to. The correspondence itself has long since been destroyed.

The cards are available online at both Ancestry (who call them 'British Army WWI Medal Rolls Index Cards') and via TNA website. Of the two, Ancestry offers by far the better reproduction in colour and provides both sides of each card, which occasionally includes the address to which the medals were sent. Basic details can be obtained free of charge, if you register, on the Lives of the First World War website at https://livesofthefirstworldwar. org/dashboard. The Medal Rolls, to which the cards refer, are at TNA in series WO 329 and transcripts of entries are online through the Naval and Military Archives, www.nmarchive.com (known here as the 'Campaign Medal Rolls'). The only additional information you are likely to discover is the infantry battalion he was serving in at the time of his death or discharge. However, this will help you find the appropriate Battalion War Diary.

Occasionally, there is other information, such as a reason for discharge or whether a man forfeited his medals because he had been a deserter. It is rare to find additional information if your man did not serve in the infantry.

Service Records: Other Ranks and Non-Commissioned Officers

Fewer than one in three service, or personnel, records for individual men survive. The remainder were destroyed during the Blitz. Even so, they are worth checking because they provide a lot of additional information.

Individual files contain a wide range of paperwork, which can be informative if at times a little bewildering, but with a little practice and patience you should be able to decipher the forms and build up an intimate portrait of the individual. They certainly repay close study.

No two files are the same. Some are very detailed with a variety of forms, letters and other paperwork. But in other cases you may only find a man's attestation form or perhaps a medical record, as is the case with Douglas Walter Belcher of the London Regiment who was awarded the Victoria Cross for bravery at St Julien in May 1915.

Of particular importance is the attestation form that was completed by the individual on enlistment. This will indicate when and where a man enlisted and was discharged and give other personal details such as civilian occupation, home address and date of birth. It usually appears at the beginning of a service record.

If a man was a pre-war regular soldier, was a part-time member of the Territorial Army or had been recalled to the colours, then the file should include his pre-war attestation form (and details of his pre-war service), which might occasionally go back to the Boer War or earlier.

11

The other form to look out for is Form B103/1, 'Casualty Form – Active Service'. Despite the name it includes far more than wounds and stays in hospital. It may tell you about: promotions through the ranks (and demotions if appropriate); list the units he served in; indicate when he went overseas and often when he returned to Britain to be discharged; details of medical treatments received; and notes of disciplinary offences (generally for drunkenness, petty theft or ignoring an officer's order). You may also find the date and reason for death or discharge. If he is discharged then there should be a reference to the appropriate sub-paragraph of King's Regulation 392 (see p. 27).

If a man died during his Army service there may well be correspondence and forms about his will and personal effects, as well as perhaps letters from the next of kin seeking more information about the circumstances of the loss of their man.

What the records will not do is to tell you very much about any fighting he was engaged in, any gallantry medals awarded or give you any real idea of his life in the Army. However, you can use the war diaries to obtain this information.

These service records are online at both Ancestry and Findmypast. They are reasonably easy to use, although you might become frustrated by the extraneous names of next of kin and children that both companies have added to make the collections seem more complete.

Records for soldiers and non-commissioned officers of the Household Cavalry (which include the Life Guards, Royal Horse Guards and Household Battalion) are available through TNA website.

The five guards regiments (Coldstream, Grenadiers, Irish, Scottish and Welsh guards) still keep their own service records, so you will need to contact the appropriate regimental headquarters at Wellington Barracks, Birdcage Walk, London SW1E 6HQ. When writing you must specify the regiment in the address. However, some guardsmen are to be found in the general collection of Army service records.

If your man continued to serve in the Army after the end of 1920 his service record is still with the Ministry of Defence. Full details are available at www.veterans-uk.info.

Army Service Numbers (Regimental Numbers)

Each ordinary soldier was given a regimental number when he enlisted. It was one of the ways he was identified in documents and on his identity tag if he was killed in action. Even today it helps considerably if you know your ancestors' service numbers, particularly if you are researching men with common names.

Until 1920 each regiment maintained its own system of numbering. When a man changed regiment, he was given a new service number. As a very rough guide, the lower his number the earlier a man enlisted. Some regimental archives have recruitment registers listing recruits in regimental number order.

In addition, regiments introduced a number of different prefixes to help differentiate the flood of new recruits in 1914 and later. The most common letter was G for General Service (that is for the duration of the war), followed by T for temporary or Territorial Army. A list of prefixes can be found at www.1914-1918.net/prefixes.html.

Incidentally, officers were not given numbers.

Officers' Service Records

Surviving service records are at TNA in two series, WO 339 and WO 374. In practice, there seems to be little difference between the two series. There is just one file for each officer. They are not online. In addition, files for a few notable individuals, including Field Marshal Lord Haig and the poet Wilfred Owen, are in series WO 138. Most records of Guards officers are still with the appropriate regimental archives.

At some stage the records were weeded and much material was destroyed. Records for men who survived are generally less full than those who died in action. Even so there may be correspondence concerning money, length of service and

Occasionally one finds letters from grieving relations in service records of both officers and other ranks. The example here is from Rudyard Kipling about his son John. (The National Archives WO 339/53917)

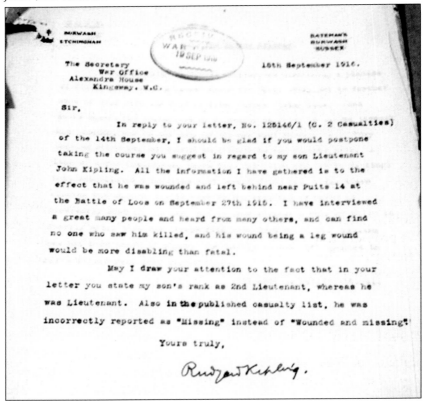

pensions, rather than about an individual's war service. If an officer came through the ranks then there should be his original enlistment document and recommendations from his commanding officer. If a man died during his service there are likely to be papers relating to the administration of his will and dispersal of his effects, as well as correspondence with the next of kin who were often trying to find out the circumstances of their son, brother or husband's death.

Officers are also listed in the Army Lists. This is an easy way to confirm whether an ancestor was an officer, because the Lists include everyone who was commissioned. They will tell which regiment or unit he was with, his rank and when he had been promoted to it. TNA has a complete set on the shelves in the Open Reading Room, and copies can be found at the Imperial War Museum, National Army Museum and some regimental museums. There are sets online available through the Internet Archive at www.archive.org and on The Genealogist website at www.thegenealogist.co.uk.

The *London Gazette* is the government's official newspaper. It includes announcements of the appointment of officers and any subsequent promotions together with when and how they were discharged. The surnames and initials of individual officers are given, together with their regiment and the date the promotion (even temporary ones) took place. Inevitably, publication may be months after the event took place, but will always give the date the promotion was granted. A brief reason for their resignation is often given. The *London Gazette* has been digitised and is online at www.thegazette.co.uk. Unfortunately, it is not terribly easy to use.

Royal Naval Division

The Royal Naval Division (RND) was initially set up to use reservists for whom there were no places on board ships, although most members were recruits who preferred to enlist in the Navy than the Army. The Division served at Gallipoli and then in Flanders, and eventually transferred to the Army as 63rd (Royal Naval) Division in 1916. Individual brigades were named after naval heroes. The RND retained many naval traditions to the intense annoyance of the Army high command, even while on land. They flew the White Ensign, used bells to signal time, used naval language (including 'going ashore' and 'coming on board' for leaving and arriving in the trenches), preferred naval ranks rather than army equivalents and sat during the toast for the King's health. Attempts to convert the RND to conform to Army practices were made but were generally unsuccessful.

Service records are online through TNA website.

The service records can be pretty informative, particularly for officers and for men killed in action. In all cases you will be given details of next of kin, date of birth and address, religion and civilian occupation together with a physical description. Within the Division the card records movements and postings and, where appropriate, a date of when they were killed.

For men who died in service, the information is largely summarised in databases to the Division's casualties, which are on both Ancestry and Findmypast.

Identifying Military Uniforms

You may have photographs of the soldiers you are researching in uniform. As well providing a direct link to the past, the insignia and badges can tell you something about his service.

Officers and other ranks wore differently designed uniforms. It is always clear which was which. Officers' uniforms were better tailored and officers were rarely seen without a tie. Ordinary soldiers wore coarser tunics and trousers (kilts, of course, in the Highland regiments). Non-commissioned officers wore downward pointing chevrons (one for a lance corporal, two for a corporal and three for a sergeant) on each arm above the elbow. They can be confused with long-service and wound stripes found below the elbow.

Each regiment and corps had its own badge worn on the cap or as buttons on the jacket and tunic. A few are very distinctive, such as the mounted gun for the Royal Artillery or the flaming grenade of the Grenadier Guards, but many are very similar.

There are various guides to help you. The best books are Neil Storey, *Military Photographs and How to Date Them* (Countryside Books, 2010) and Robert Pols, *Identifying Old Army Photographs* (Family History Partnership, 2011). For regimental badges see Ian Swinnerton, *Identifying Your World War I Soldier from Badges and Photographs* (Family History Partnership, 2004) and Peter Doyle and Chris Foster, *British Army Cap Badges of the First World War* (Shire, 2010).

Probably the best general introduction to interpreting uniforms is provided by Chris McDonald at www.4thgordons. com/I-Spybook%20of%20Uniforms1.2.pdf. There are several rather unsatisfactory sites to help identify regimental badges: the best is probably the British Armed Services and National Service site at www.britisharmedforces. org/index.php.

Chapter 3

CASUALTIES

Introduction

Just over 700,000 British men and a few dozen women were killed during the First World War, and many hundreds of thousands more received some form of medical treatment. Some 150,000 of these still lie in the Ypres Salient.

Every British and Commonwealth soldier who died during the First World War is commemorated in some way by the Commonwealth War Graves Commission. The Commission was set up in May 1917 to commemorate the dead of the First World War. By the Armistice, 587,000 graves had been identified and a further 559,000 casualties were registered as having no known grave. Even today bodies are still being recovered.

The Commission is perhaps best known for the hundreds of carefully tended, and very moving, cemeteries scattered through Northern France and Belgium, although it maintains cemeteries in 150 countries across the world. You can find a lot more about its work and its history on its website at www.cwgc.org.

The Commission's database of war deaths is also on the website. It is one of the key resources for First World War research and is very easy to use. You can search by name, regiment or cemetery or filter searches by service, nationality or year of death.

For each individual the Register will tell you: the name that appears on the gravestone or the memorial if his body was never identified; the date of his death; his age (if known) and nationality; rank, service number (if appropriate) and the unit to which he belonged; the cemetery and the plot number where he is buried or

In Memory of

Private

Hyman Costa

43606, 9th Bn., Royal Inniskilling Fusiliers who died on 12 May 1917 Age 37

Son of Raphael and Rachael Costa; husband of Hannah Costa, of 62, Chippenham Rd., Maida Hill, London.

Remembered with Honour
Dranoutre Military Cemetery

Commemorated in perpetuity by
the Commonwealth War Graves Commission

On the Commonwealth War Graves Commission website you can download a certificate containing most of the information they have about individual soldiers. The information supplied by relatives can be very helpful if you wish to trace the man's family. (Commonwealth War Graves Commission)

for men who have no known grave, the panel on the appropriate memorial to the missing on which his name has been engraved.

Often there are notes about his parents or wife, any special inscription chosen by the family for his grave, or perhaps whether he was attached to another regiment at the time of death. The family supplied this additional information as the Commission contacted relatives to give them the opportunity to add personal details. For Private Hyman Costa, 9th Royal Inniskilling Fusiliers, who was killed on 12 May 1917 and now lies in Dranoutre Military Cemetery, the additional entry reads: 'Age 37. Son of Raphael and Rachael Costa; husband of Hannah Costa of 62 Chippenham Rd. Maida Hill London.' Occasionally, the details are more profound. For Second Lieutenant Arthur Conway Young, Royal Inniskilling Fusiliers, who was killed on 16 August 1917 and is buried at Tyne Cot, the inscription on his grave bitterly reads, 'Born at Kobe Japan 9th October 1890 sacrificed to the fallacy that war can end war'. Interestingly, the inscription does not appear in the Commission's paperwork for the man.

There may also be Grave Registration Reports providing basic details of the individuals, such as name, service number, rank, regiment, unit and date of death, together with Headstone Documents which detail what was actually inscribed on an individual's headstone. For Hyman Costa there is a note that he was Jewish, so instead of the normal cross there is a Star of David on his grave.

There are one or two pitfalls. The most common of which is how individual men are described. Sometimes an individual is only identified by their initials or forename. Private Douglas Tyler, 10th Sherwood Foresters, for example, who was killed on 14 December 1915, is referred to as A. D. Tyler. So you may need to do a search by surname.

The exact location of a grave in any Commonwealth War Graves Commission cemetery is indicated by a Roman numeral following the entry, the row by a capital letter and the grave by a number. Thus II. B. 28 indicates plot II, row B, grave 28. In the registers of cemeteries that are not divided into plots the row is indicated by a capital letter following the entry and the grave by a number. Thus D. 12 indicates Row D, Grave 12.

It is possible to obtain photographs of war graves, without visiting the cemetery, by contacting the War Graves Photographic Project via http://twgpp.org. The website includes an index which allows you to see whether there is already a photo of the grave you are interested in. If there is, you can call up a low-resolution image of the gravestone. You can also obtain a high-resolution image of the stone for a donation. They recommend a very reasonable £3.50. More details are of course on the website.

Soldiers Died in the Great War

More information can often be found in the Soldiers Died in the Great War databases, available through both Ancestry and Findmypast. The War Office originally compiled these records in the early 1920s. Soldiers Died contains additional details to that provided by the Commonwealth War Graves Commission, notably the place and date of enlistment and home address.

Information listed about an individual may include: name, rank and number; birthplace; where they enlisted; home town; regiment and battalion; type of casualty, usually 'killed in action', but sometimes 'died of wounds'; date of death; theatre of war where the individual died, generally Western Europe. Occasionally, a place of death is also given.

The Name List

The In Flanders Fields Museum in Ypres has details of about 600,000 men from all sides who died in Flanders during the First World War. The information is fairly brief and is based on information provided by the Commonwealth War Graves

Commission and its sister organisations. Still, it really brings it home that men from many nations lost their lives in the bloodbath that was the Ypres Salient. Details can be found at www.inflandersfields.be/en/knowledge-center/casualty-database/introduction.

Missing in Action

If you are researching an individual for whom there is no known grave it is worth seeing whether his disappearance was reported to the International Committee of the Red Cross in Geneva. If it was, there may be a card for him, which will give details of when and where he was reported missing, his unit and the company he was in, together with details of next of kin. Occasionally, there may be a note of his fate, whether he survived to become a prisoner of war or died of wounds while in German hands. These records are online at http://grandeguerre.icrc.org. Armed with this information then you can turn to the war diaries for a description of how and why he went missing.

Casualty Lists

From the beginning of the war the War Office published daily lists of casualties, both lists of men killed and those wounded. The lists of deaths in particular was picked up by many newspapers.

The information given is basic, just name, rank and unit, together with their home town. No dates are given of when a man was killed or wounded, but you can assume that the events took place four to six weeks before the information was published in the Casualty Lists. Hyman Costa, for example, was killed on 12 May 1917, but appears in the List published on 26 June, while Sergeant Sidney Ruck was killed on 8 May 1915 and is in the List of 7 June.

An incomplete set of Lists is available on The Genealogist website at www.thegenealogist.co.uk, and many were published in *The Times* and other newspapers.

Rolls of Honour

One phenomenon of the War was the roll of honour: a published list of the deceased (and occasionally other groups of servicemen such as prisoners of war). Rolls are often available for workplaces (such as local councils and railway companies), chapels and small communities. They are definitely worth looking out for, although in most cases the information they contain can as easily be obtained from the Commonwealth War Graves Commission or Soldiers Died in the Great War databases.

There is no nationwide set of these rolls, although the Imperial War Museum and British Library almost certainly have the largest collections. And a good many are with the Society of Genealogists in London. Archives and local study libraries may have copies of ones for their area. A number have been republished by the Naval & Military Press (www.naval-military-press.com).

There are several larger national rather than local rolls. Entries for some 26,000 officers and other ranks (including 7,000 photographs) were collected and published in 1917 by the Marquis Melville de Ruvigny, a noted genealogist of the period. De Ruvigny's *Roll of Honour: A Biographical Record of His Majesty's Military and Aerial Forces Who Fell in the Great War 1914–1917* is available on Ancestry and Findmypast.

If you are researching Irish soldiers it is worth looking at Ireland's Memorial Records of the Great War, which is available on Ancestry, the Naval and Military Archive and Findmypast's Irish website at www.findmypast.ie. A random selection of rolls of honour is available at www.roll-of-honour.com.

War Memorials

After the war some tens of thousands of war memorials were erected in honour of men who did not return. They are still common features in towns and villages. As well as those commemorating the dead from a particular town or area, there are many memorials for schools, churches or work places.

An individual may appear on several town or parish memorials, or in rare cases may have been missed off altogether either because the organisers forgot or the family did not want the man to be so commemorated. Normally, all you will find is his surname and Christian name or initials, sometimes the rank and unit and details of gallantry medals are also included.

The UK National Inventory of War Memorials, at the Imperial War Museum, has prepared a database of some 55,000 memorials at www.ukniwm.org.uk. This number includes 958 specifically dedicated to the men who fell at Ypres and another 518 for men who died in Flanders, including Douglas Tyler who was killed in action on 14 December 1915, and is commemorated in a memorial at All Saints Church in Mackworth, Derbyshire. Unusually, there is a milepost outside Christ Church, Shooters Hill in south-east London indicating that it is 130 miles from there to Ypres. It says: 'In Defending The Salient/Our Casualties/Were/90,000 Killed/70,500 Missing/ 410,000 Wounded'.

The results can include a full transcript of the dedication and a physical description of the memorial and an account of why and how it came to be created. Sometimes there is a photograph as well. And an increasing number of entries include listings of all the individuals to be found commemorated on the memorial.

If you are researching an Irish soldier then check out the Irish War Memorials website (www.irishwarmemorials.ie) which lists many memorials to the fallen in both the North and South, and there are indexes both to individuals and places.

Scotland's war dead are honoured at the Scots National War Memorial at Edinburgh Castle. More information can be found at www.snwm.org.

Hospital Records

If the service record for your man survives it should contain a Casualty Form (Form B103) which records visits to the doctor, admission to hospital and so on. Of course, many entries refer to war-related wounds, but a surprising number of entries concern normal ailments and complaints. The forms can sometimes be difficult to decode because they also contain details of postings, promotions and demotions, as well as punishments.

An efficient system for dealing with casualties was quickly introduced at the outbreak of war to ferry the sick and wounded to the appropriate casualty clearing station or hospital in the rear. A card was compiled for each man, but all these records (with the exception of a small sample) have long been destroyed. A limited and unindexed selection of records is in MH 106 at TNA. This material is slowly going online at Forces Records.

If you know which hospital they were in when the returned to Britain, it may also be worth checking the online database of hospital records (www.nationalarchives.gov.uk/hospitalrecords) to see whether anything survives at local archives or with the hospital itself.

Sue Light has created an excellent guide to medical records at www.scarletfinders.co.uk/125.htm.

Silver War Badge

The Silver War Badge was instituted in 1916. It was a small, circular lapel badge made of sterling silver, which bore the King's initials, a crown, and the inscriptions 'For King and Empire' and 'Services Rendered'. The Badge provided former soldiers with some form of identification to show that they had faithfully served King and Country. Medal Rolls are available on Ancestry, but they are not very informative. Perhaps of more use are the transcripts held by the Naval and Military Archives, if for no other reason than that they will give the reason for discharge as outlined in paragraph 392 of the King's Regulations (see p. 27).

Generally, only the cause for discharge is given in the Medal Rolls, such as 'wounds' or 'injuries', together with the date of discharge. Occasionally, you may find the date of enlistment as well.

Criteria for Discharge

On service records, Medal Index Cards and the registers of the Silver War Badge you may come across a set of abbreviations, perhaps something like K.R. 392 (xvi). This refers to paragraph 392 of the 1912 edition of the King's Regulations, which governed how the British Army was to be administered. The paragraph contained all the official causes of discharge, which were set out in a series sub-paragraphs. The vast majority of men were discharged in respect of sub-paragraph xvi, as being 'No longer physically fit for war service'.

The criteria for discharge were:

(i) References on enlistment being unsatisfactory
(ii) Having been irregularly enlisted
(iii) Not likely to become an efficient soldier (with sub clauses as below)
  (a) Recruit rejected both by Medical Officer and Approving Officer
  (b) Recruit passed by Medical Officer, but rejected by a Recruiting Officer stationed away from the headquarters of the recruiting area, or by Approving Officer
  (c) Recruit within three months of enlistment considered unfit for service
    (cc) Recruits with more than three months service considered unfit for further military service
  (d) Recruit who after having undergone a course of physical training is recommended by an examining board to be

discharged, or in the case of a mounted corps is unable to ride

(e) Soldier of local battalion abroad considered unlikely to become efficient

(f) Boy who, on reaching 18 years of age, is considered to be physically unfit for the ranks

(iv) Having been claimed as an apprentice

(v) Having claimed it on payment of £10 within three months of his attestation

(vi) Having made a mis-statement as to age on enlistment (with sub clauses as below)

(a) Soldier under 17 years of age at date of application for discharge

(b) Soldier between 17 and 18 years of age at date of application for discharge

(vii) Having been claimed for wife desertion (with sub clauses as below)

(a) By the parish authorities

(b) By the wife

(viii) Having made a false answer on attestation

(ix) Unfitted for the duties of the corps

(x) Having been convicted by the civil power of a specific offence, such as rape or murder, or of an offence committed before enlistment

(xi) For misconduct

(xii) Having been sentenced to penal servitude

(xiii) Having been sentenced to be discharged with ignominy

(xiv) At his own request, on payment of a specified amount under Article 1130 (i), Pay Warrant

(xv) Free, after a specific number of years' service under Article 1130 (ii), Pay Warrant (with sub clauses as below)

(xva) Free under Article 1130 (i), Pay Warrant

(xvb) Free to take up civil employment which cannot be held open

(xvi) No longer physically fit for war service

(xvia) Surplus to military requirements (having suffered impairment since entry into the service)

(xvii) – paragraph not used

(xviii) At his own request after 18 years service (with a view to pension under the Pay Warrant)

(xix) For the benefit of the public service after 18 years service (with a view to pension under the Pay Warrant)

(xx) Inefficiency after 18 years service (with a view to pension under the Pay Warrant)

(xxi) The termination of his period of engagement

(xxii) With less than 21 years service towards engagement, but with 21 or more years service towards pension

(xxiii) Having claimed discharge after three months' notice

(xxiv) Having reached the age for discharge

(xxv) His services being no longer required

  (a) Surplus to military requirements (not having suffered impairment since entry into the service)

(xxvi) At his own request after 21 (or more) years service (with a view to pension under the Pay Warrant)

(xxvii) After 21 (or more) years qualifying service for pension, and with 5 (or more) years service as warrant officer (with a view to pension under the Pay Warrant)

(xxxviii) On demobilisation

Chapter 4

GALLANTRY MEDALS

Gallantry medals were awarded for acts of heroism and bravery on the field of battle. Some medals were awarded immediately for special acts (sometimes referred to as being awarded 'in the field'), while others – known as non-immediate – might be awarded weeks or months after the act.

The most prestigious gallantry medal is the Victoria Cross. Biographies of the 633 men who won the award during the First World War, together with descriptions of their exploits, are described by Gerald Gliddon in an excellent series of books, published by The History Press. There are also several websites devoted to VC winners, although Wikipedia, which has biographies of each man, is probably the best place to start. A register of VC winners can be found in series WO 98 at TNA, together with copies of their citations and other information is also available online on Discovery.

The Distinguished Service Order (DSO) was normally only awarded to senior officers, while the Military Cross (MC) was awarded for acts of bravery to officers of the rank of captain or below. The equivalents for non-commissioned officers and other ranks were the Distinguished Conduct Medal (DCM) and Military Medal (MM).

In many cases non-immediate gallantry awards were given out almost randomly to members of a platoon or company who had seen action. Often men were asked to nominate comrades who should be honoured.

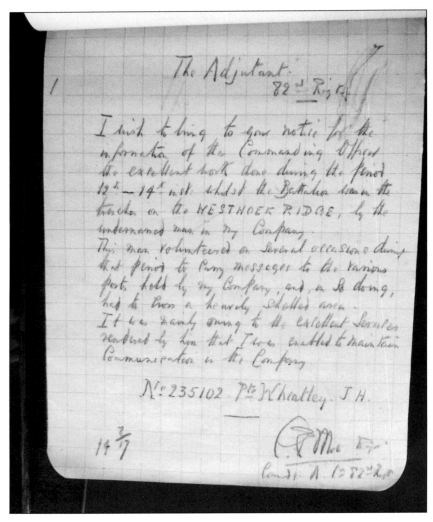

It can be hard to find very much about the award of gallantry medals. Occasionally there might be material in the war diaries, or here in a note recommending the award of a Military Medal to Private James Harold Wheatley, South Lancashire Regiment. The award was gazetted on 16 October 1917. Wheatley eventually was commissioned in the London Regiment and survived the war. (Author/Lancashire Infantry Museum)

If there isn't a family story about the award of a gallantry medal, or the medal itself, you may find a note on the Medal Index Card or, more rarely, in the service record.

Details of all gallantry awards were published in the *London Gazette*. For the higher awards there should be a citation, that is a short description of why the medal was awarded. For Lance Sergeant Douglas Walter Belcher, 1/5 London Regiment, who won a Victoria Cross just north of Ypres the entry in the *London Gazette* for 22 June 1915 reads:

> On the early morning of 13 May 1915 when in charge of a portion of an advanced breastwork south of the Wieltje–St Julien Road during a very fierce and continuous bombardment by the enemy, which frequently blew in the breastwork, Lance Sergeant Belcher with a mere handful of men elected to remain and endeavour to hold his position after the troops near him had been withdrawn. By his skill and great gallantry he maintained his position during the day, opening rapid fire on the enemy who were only 100 to 150 yards distant, whenever he saw them collecting for an attack. There is little doubt that the bold front shown by Lance Sergeant Belcher prevented the enemy from breaking through on the Wieltje Road and averted an attack on one of our Divisions.

At the very least the *London Gazette* entry will give you the man's name, service number (not officers), rank, regiment and the date when the award was made. For awards of the MM and Mentions in Despatches (MiD) this is the only information you are likely to find.

However, it can be fairly hard to find out anything else about how and why medals were won. The paperwork appears largely to have been destroyed during the Blitz. In particular you will not find anything about MiD apart from the entry in the *London*

Gazette. However, if you are lucky, you may be able to find something in the unit war diaries. Generally, there are entries recording the award of gallantry medals to officers and, less frequently, other ranks, without giving the reason why. You might also want to look at the war diary for the brigade in which the battalion found itself, as awards had to be approved by the Brigade's commanding officer.

Citations for awards of the Distinguished Conduct Medal (DCM) can be found on both Ancestry and Findmypast. They usually duplicate what appears in the *London Gazette* but are certainly easier to find.

There are also some Medal Index Cards for men awarded the DCM and MM. They give you little more than the date and page number in the *London Gazette* where the award is listed. In my experience the date given is often wrong.

The Genealogist (www.thegenealogist.co.uk) has a set of cards of Military Medal winners, which give the date the award appeared in the *London Gazette*. Occasionally, other information is given such as the award of an additional Military Medal ('a bar' in Army parlance). In addition, Findmypast has a list of Artillerymen who won the Military Medal with the date their award was gazetted. In both cases the dates of publication in the *London Gazette* could be a few days out due to a backlog of entries waiting to be published.

The award of gallantry medals awards may well feature in newspaper stories.

The most common award was the Mention in Despatches (MiD) for acts of bravery or service that warranted reward, but was not enough to merit a gallantry award. During the war just over 2 per cent of the men in the British forces (141,082 officers and other ranks) were so honoured, and recipients were listed in the *London Gazette*. The fact that a man was awarded a MiD is usually shown on the Medal Index Card (often abbreviated to EM or EMB with a date when the award was published in the *Gazette*).

There may also be separate cards with the approximate date the award was gazetted.

Further Reading
More about medals (both gallantry and campaign) can be found in Peter Duckers, *British Military Medals: a Guide for Collectors and Researchers* (2nd edn, Pen & Sword, 2013). Also useful is the *Medals Yearbook* published by Token Publishing annually.

Chapter 5

COURTS MARTIAL

Nearly 300,000 soldiers and 6,000 officers faced courts martial during the war, generally for being absent without leave, petty theft or drunkenness. The Casualty Form in the service record will record misdemeanours and should indicate whether your ancestor was put on a charge. Registers of courts martial in WO 90 (for men serving overseas) and WO 92 (for men on home duty) give brief details of the offences. Details of more serious offences can be found in registers in WO 213 with a few files in WO 71 (including for those unfortunate men who were 'Shot at Dawn' for desertion and other offences) and WO 93.

Chapter 6

PRISONERS OF WAR

Nearly 193,000 British and Commonwealth prisoners of war fell into the hands of the Germans and their allies during the war, about half of whom were captured during the last 6 months of the war. Conditions could be grim, often because of increasing problems within Germany itself, rather than any deliberately policy to mistreat prisoners. Many men eventually came to depend largely on Red Cross parcels, which were collected and packed by voluntary organisations under the leadership of the British Red Cross.

The International Committee of the Red Cross (ICRC) in Geneva was responsible for passing details of prisoners of war between the various combatant nations and ensuring that conditions in the camps were adequate. The Committee collected, analysed and classified information it received from the detaining powers and national agencies about prisoners of war and civilian internees. It compared this information with requests submitted to it by relatives or friends, in order to restore contact between them. The Agency's collections consist of some 500,000 pages of lists and 6 million index cards, which can be extremely informative. They are now online at http://grandeguerre.icrc.org. The records will tell you when and where a man was taken prisoner, the camps he was in and details of his next of kin back in Britain, and perhaps when they were repatriated home or sent to Switzerland for recuperation. If they died while in German hands there may be a note about the date and place of death and where they were buried. There are also some cards for men reported missing. In addition, there are some reports about conditions in individual camps written in French or German.

However, it is difficult to find out very much about individual POWs in British archives, as the records have largely been destroyed. A list of prisoners in German and Turkish hands in 1916 can be found in piece AIR 1/892/204/5/696-698, at Kew which indicates where a prisoner was captured and when, where they were held and their next of kin. There is a published List of Officers taken Prisoner in the Various Theatres of War between August 1914 and November 1918 (1919, repr. 1988) online at Findmypast.

Returning British prisoners were interrogated by the authorities about their experiences and surviving reports (some 3,000 in total) can be downloaded from TNA's website. Officers were interrogated about the circumstances of their capture and reports can be found in their service records.

Further Reading
Paterson, Sarah, *Tracing Your First World War Prisoners of War*, Pen & Sword, 2012
van Emden, Richard, *Prisoners of the Kaiser,* Pen & Sword, 2009

Chapter 7

PENSIONS

Widows and disabled ex-servicemen were entitled to claim a pension. Much ill-feeling was created by the low level of the pension and the difficulties placed in the way of claimants by the government and local officials supervising the grant of awards. Most records have long since been destroyed. However, series PIN 82 at TNA contains an 8 per cent sample of widows' and dependents' papers arranged in alphabetical order. The forms give personal details of each serviceman's name, place of residence, particulars of service and the date, place and cause of death or injury. They also give details of the assessment of, and entitlement to, pensions awards, the amount awarded and the length of time for which the award was granted.

There is a set of post-First World War pension appeal records at the National Records of Scotland (www.nrscotland.gov.uk) in series PT6. The records contain detailed pension applications from thousands of Scottish soldiers and their next of kin (usually widows).

The Western Front Association (WFA) recently rescued a series of pension cards relating to the payment of pensions and other payments to soldiers and their dependents. As with all records of the First World War, the content varies greatly between individuals but you can expect to find material about the individual and his family as well as the reason why payments were made. At present the records are being indexed by the Association, but they will do look-ups for enquires for a small fee. You can find out more at www.westernfrontassociation.com /great-war-current-news/pension-records.html.

Chapter 8

PERSONAL PAPERS AND EFFECTS

Soldiers (and indeed for that matter sailors and airmen) wrote about their experiences at the time in letters and diaries and perhaps in old age they wrote up their memoirs. An increasing number are appearing in print, on websites or in TV and radio programmes. That they did this is not surprising: they were witnessing events unique in human history.

There was a very efficient postal service. Most soldiers took advantage of this, scribbling regular letters home. Because of censorship and the wish not to frighten their families, these letters tend to be fairly anodyne, reassuring the reader that they are well, perhaps indicating that they are safe behind the lines and asking for items to be sent out. In general they are not great works of literature, but even so after nearly a century they are treasured family heirlooms.

Neither officers nor men were allowed to keep diaries, although clearly many did. Some were just simple entries about the weather and where he was stationed noted in a pocket diary. Others were much more elaborate affairs.

Memoirs are also important. Some are based on diaries and letters or correspondence with old comrades, while others were clearly written decades later for the grandchildren or to excise old ghosts.

Or you might just have his medals, army service discharge paper, pay book or photographs. Or indeed no records at all, except perhaps vague family memories.

If you have such a collection it is well worth considering donating it to the Imperial War Museum or a local record office or regimental archive. They may be willing to give you a set of copies in return for the originals. Certainly you should think about making some provision for their care in your will.

There is no central list of what personal papers are to be found where, although it is worth checking the National Register of Archives to see whether they have details of any such collections of papers (www.nationalarchives.gov.uk/nra).

The Imperial War Museum has the most important collection of personal papers. Many are described on the Museum's catalogue at www.iwm.org.uk/collections/search.

Another important resource is the Liddle Collection at Leeds University's Brotherton Library which has over 4,000 collections of private papers. Details can be found at http://library.leeds.ac.uk/liddle-collection.

Regimental archives and the National Army Museum are also good sources of information. The Royal Artillery Archives in Woolwich, for example, has much for the First World War, particularly for officers. In addition, small collections can sometimes be found at local record offices.

Lastly, an increasing number of diaries and memoirs in particular are being published or appearing online. Pen & Sword has published well over a hundred such titles, which you can buy direct at www.pen-and-sword.co.uk, such as Frank Vans Agnew's *Veteran Volunteer*, Edwin Vaughan's *Some Desperate Glory* and Harry Owen's *A Doctor on the Western Front*. Many others are available from the Naval & Military Press (www.naval-military-press.com).

The Imperial War Museum and other museums have impressive collections of ephemera. In the case of the IWM, this can be seen in its online catalogue and much of it is displayed in the impressive new galleries at the Museum's London and Manchester sites.

A fascinating Europe-wide initiative to collect personal items from each of the participating nations is being collated by Europeana at www.europeana1914-1918.eu/en. It brings home the often forgotten fact that the war was fought by nations other than Britain and the British Empire.

Chapter 9

OTHER USEFUL
GENEALOGICAL RECORDS

It is easy to overlook the basic genealogical sources of birth, marriage and death records, census returns and wills in researching soldiers, but they are also worth checking out. And of course many researchers first become aware of having military ancestors from an entry in the census or on a marriage certificate.

Most of these records are now available online, or likely to become so in the foreseeable future.

The Census

Census records are an important source for family history revealing unique information about ancestors. In particular, because it was taken so close to the outbreak of the war, the 1911 census is a key source. The English and Welsh census is available through Findmypast and Ancestry. It is easy to find Hyman Costa's 1911 census entry because the information is given in his Commonwealth War Graves Commission papers. It reveals that he had a baby daughter called Rachel Ray and was a 'fruit salesman' or costermonger by trade.

The Scottish 1911 census is at ScotlandsPeople (www. scotlandspeople.gov.uk) and the Irish census is at www. census.nationalarchives.ie. The information in all three censuses is almost identical and they are fully indexed.

The 1911 census is unique for another reason. For the first time servicemen, and their families, serving overseas in both the Navy and Army were recorded. Soldier's names, age, rank and place of birth were recorded. Of particular interest are the returns for Army wives and children. To access the military returns in the appropriate box on the search screen tick 'Overseas military'.

Birth, Marriage and Death Certificates

National registration began in England and Wales on 1 July 1837 (Scotland – 1855, Ireland – 1864). The system has remained largely unchanged since then. You can order certificates for men who were killed in action or died of wounds during the war. However, there is little point as they don't tell you anything you don't know already.

English and Welsh certificates can be ordered online at www.gro.gov.uk/gro/content/certificates/default.asp or by phone on 0300 123 1837. Scottish ones are all online through Scotland's People. Indexes to Irish births, marriages and deaths for the period (both North and South) are available through FamilySearch (www.familysearch.org), but you have to order the certificates from the General Register Office for Ireland (www.groireland.ie).

Also of interest are Chaplains' Returns and Army Register Books recording births, baptisms, marriages, deaths and burials of soldiers and their families at home and abroad. Indexes are at www.findmypast.com and at TNA in Kew.

TNA also holds a small number of regimental registers of births, baptisms, marriages and burials in series WO 156, which are online at Deceased Online (www.deceasedonline.co.uk).

Wills

It was natural for soldiers to make wills before going into action. Indeed, the Army pay book, which was issued to all soldiers, included a simple will form which could be completed. Generally, any possessions were left to the individual's wife or next of kin.

There may well be papers about wills and the disposal of personal effects in the files of individual officers and soldiers. If an individual made a will that was proved in the Principal Probate Registry, then details were published in the National Probate Calendars. The Calendars are online at Ancestry. Wills themselves cost £10 (at the time of writing) and can be ordered by post from the Leeds District Probate Registry, York House, 31 York Place, Leeds LS1 2BA.

In addition the Probate Registry has released some 200,000 wills that were made by soldiers in the field. There is an index at www.gov.uk/probate-search. Again, you can order copies online for £10 each.

The National Records of Scotland has a collection of 30,000 wills for Scottish soldiers. There is an online index, although you can only see digital images of the originals in the reading rooms. For more details see www.nas.gov.uk/guides/searchSoldiers Wills.asp. The Irish National Archives has some 9,000 wills available at http://soldierswills.nationalarchives.ie/search/sw/home.jsp.

Chapter 10

RESEARCHING UNITS

Structure

During the First World War the British Army expanded from a fairly small organisation in July 1914 to a huge institution by the end of 1918, which historians have suggested was the biggest organisation ever created in Britain. During the war 5.7 million British and Irish men served in the Army at some stage. Or to put it another way, rather more than 20 per cent of the adult male population wore khaki. The vast majority of these men served overseas. In addition, another 3 million from the Empire (of whom half were Indian) also saw service. They had to be equipped, fed and trained before being sent into the fighting. It always amazes me that this expansion took place without a major hiccup and yet is so little known about today. The one serious exception was the shell shortage of the spring and summer of 1915, which seriously affected British plans to go on the offensive in the Ypres Salient. Recalling his days as a staff officer in 1917, Arthur Behrends wrote:

> We in France and Flanders in 1917 and 1918 had no complaints about the way in which we were administered. Our medical, transport and supply services had advanced a lot since the days of the Boer and Crimean wars. We were well fed and clothed, when we were wounded or sick we were admirably looked after, leave was given fairly regularly; during my time with the BEF there was no

shortage of guns or ammunition, motors, maps or anything. To us it seemed that the vast if at times cumbersome machine worked smoothly, and to us it was the last word in modernity.

The structure of the Army throughout the war remained fairly simple and logical, although the terminology may occasionally be confusing and there are lots of exceptions. The paragraphs below are just a brief overview, and more detail is available on the Long, Long Trail website. In particular, the Army used the word 'Corps' in several different ways. Corps lay below Armies and above Divisions in the Army command structure (see below). The specialist arms, such as the Royal Artillery and Royal Engineers, were also formed into Corps. And lastly there was the King's Royal Rifle Corps, an infantry regiment.

The British Expeditionary Force (BEF), as the British Army on the Western Front was known, was divided in December 1914 into a number of armies, each of which was responsible for a specific sector of the Front. In Flanders it was the First and Second Armies, although the Second Army spent a few months in Italy over the winter of 1917/18.

Initially command of the BEF was given to Sir John French. In December 1915 he was replaced by Sir Douglas Haig. French and Haig were ultimately under the control of the War Cabinet in London. Herbert Asquith, who was Prime Minister between August 1914 and December 1916, was largely content to allow the generals to manage the war as they saw fit. This was not a view taken by David Lloyd George when he succeeded Asquith in December 1916. Lloyd George increasingly lost faith in Haig and his generals' ability to win the war without huge numbers of casualties. And his reduction of British forces on the Western Front during the winter of 1917 – in order to reinforce the Italian Front – was a significant factor in the success of the German advance in March and April 1918.

Each army was composed of an Army HQ which commanded at least two corps, with various units attached as army troops. In turn, the Army HQ reported to General Headquarters in St Omer or, from 1916, in the attractive French town of Montreuil-sur-Mer.

Below them the corps replicated to an extent the structures of the armies above them. They too had units of army troops attached to their headquarters. And in turn they were responsible for two or more divisions. Eventually twenty-two infantry corps were established, together with separate corps for the cavalry, Australians and New Zealanders (ANZAC), Canadians and Indians.

Army or Corps HQs were generally permanently based in a chateau or similar, 15 to 20 miles behind the front line. Numbers of headquarters staff were surprisingly small. Both armies and corps were responsible for staff work, that is planning battles and ensuring that the troops were properly provisioned. The men in the front line had a particular dislike of staff officers, whom they regarded as being out of touch with the realities of trench warfare.

Divisions were the highest echelons that were actively engaged in action. They were responsible for implementing the orders sent from Corps and Army HQs. As a result they were the highest unit to which the ordinary soldier had affinity with. They were made up of a number of infantry battalions and divisional troops consisting of units of artillery, engineers, hospitals, and, from 1916, machine-gunners, together with a small headquarters. Very roughly each division was made up of about 20,000 men from 3 brigades. The divisions were constantly on the move along the Western Front. In addition, battalions joined and left depending on tactical needs or the shortage of troops.

Below them lay the brigades, which were made up of four battalions, a headquarters and brigade troops. They should not be confused with Royal Artillery brigades, which were equivalent to regiments (and indeed were so renamed just before the Second World War).

But the most important fighting unit was the infantry battalion, which at full strength consisted of about 1,000 men. Battalions were part of a regiment, which through the regimental depot was responsible for recruiting and training men (at least initially), and through the wives of senior officers for organising support for men who had been taken prisoner of war and widows of those who had fallen. Among other duties the depot would also keep the regimental archives and ephemera and publish the regimental magazine.

From 1881 regiments, with the exception of the Rifle Brigade and King's Royal Rifle Corps, were linked to particular counties or cities. The affiliation is often clear from the regimental title, such as the King's Liverpool Regiment or the East Surreys. In peacetime the regiment would recruit from the communities in their area, but of course men might choose to join another regiment other than their local one. Local recruiting continued until the introduction of conscription in March 1916 when conscripts began to be assigned to the regiments at random (although volunteers could still choose the regiment they wished to serve with). In addition, units might well be broken up and men drafted to units that had been badly affected by losses in battle. The East End costermonger Hyman Costa, who originally enlisted in the Royal Fusiliers (which recruited in London), must have felt very strange when he was transferred to the Royal Inniskilling Regiment, whose battalions largely consisted of men from the rural counties of Donegal, Fermanagh and Tyrone. Unit War Diaries sometimes record the arrival of new drafts of men, occasionally with comments on their quality, but almost never give their names.

In peacetime the regiment was made up of two battalions of regular soldiers, one of whom was normally based in Great Britain or Ireland, while the other was overseas, generally in India. In addition, the Third and Fourth battalions were territorial units made up of part-time soldiers. On the outbreak of war in 1914 there was a huge expansion of the Army as men flocked to the

A drawing of men opening tins of rations. Although the diet was monotonous, men were generally well fed, particularly in comparison with the Germans. (Author)

colours. New infantry battalions were created almost on a daily basis. Some territorial battalions were split to form cadres for new units. In some regiments these were simply sequentially numbered (typically 6th and 7th) but in others they were given a number which showed their ancestry, i.e. if the 5th King's Own Yorkshire Light Infantry was split the two resulting battalions were numbered 1/5th and 2/5th. Other battalions raised for the war were known as service battalions. These took their numbers immediately after the original territorial battalions. The Hampshire Regiment, for example, eventually had nineteen battalions.

An infantry battalion was made up of a Battalion Headquarters Company and four companies. The battalion was usually commanded by a Lieutenant-Colonel, with a Major as second-in-command. In addition, at Battalion HQ would be the adjutant, who was in charge of battalion administration, including writing up the war diary; a quartermaster responsible for stores and transport; and a medical officer, who was on detachment from the RAMC.

Here you would also find the Regimental Sergeant-Major (RSM), the most senior non-commissioned officer as well as a number of specialist roles filled by sergeants, including quartermasters, cooks, signallers and the orderly room clerk. There were also a number of specialist sections, such as the signallers (who were sometimes men being groomed as potential officers), machine-gunners (although in January 1916 they were transferred to the new Machine Gun Corps), drivers for the horse-drawn transport, and stretcher-bearers who traditionally were the musicians of the battalion band.

As well as the Battalion HQ there were four companies, generally given letters A–D. Each company was commanded by a Major or Captain. In addition, there was a Company Sergeant-Major (CSM) and the 'quarterbloke', the Company Quartermaster Sergeant (CQMS).

In turn companies were divided into four platoons, under lieutenants and second lieutenants, sometimes referred to as subalterns. And again each platoon consisted of four sections. Generally, each section comprised twelve men under an NCO. These were the men that an ordinary soldier would work with, fight with and socialise with. A private might also have dealings with the platoon commander and perhaps knew the company and battalion commanders by sight.

In some ways the organisation of the battalion was similar to that of a secondary school. If you think back to your time at school you would know the form teacher and others who taught you, but might know only by sight the head teacher and heads of subjects. And the chances are that you would spend most of your day with a small group of friends who were in the same class as you.

Although the majority of men serving in Flanders would have been in infantry units, by the end of the war the proportion of men at 'the sharp end', in Winston Churchill's memorable phrase, was declining fast. There were a number of specialist services or arms, such as the Royal Artillery, Royal Engineers and Royal Army Medical Corps. Fortunately, the records are much the same, although it can be almost impossible to identify which particular unit a gunner, sapper, driver or stretcher-bearer served with.

In particular the British Army was becoming much more mechanised. Even if the tactics and uniforms had changed the British Expeditionary Force of 1914 would have been clearly recognisable to the men who fought at Waterloo a century previously. But by 1918 the Army was a very different institution. The most obvious example of this is perhaps the tank. These land ships or land crabs, as they were initially called, arrived on the Western Front in the autumn of 1916 and caused panic among enemy soldiers, but they were first used with real success at the Battle of Cambrai in October 1917. Tanks really came into their

A scene somewhere on the Ypres Salient which well conveys the horrors of the war. (Author)

own during the advances of the 'Hundred Days' between August and November 1918. They provided much of the support to allow the infantry to advance through German lines. Originally, tanks came under the responsibilities of the Machine Gun Corps, but a separate Tank Corps was established in July 1917.

The most important of these separate specialist arms was the Royal Artillery. Artillery, and its use, was key to the eventual Allied victory. The military historian John Terraine, in his 1982 book *White Heat – the new warfare 1914–18,* argues that: 'The war of 1914–18 was an artillery war: artillery was the battle-winner, artillery was what caused the greatest loss of life, the most dreadful wounds, and the deepest fear.' The BEF crossed the Channel in August 1914 with twenty-four 5in guns. By the Armistice Sir Douglas Haig had 6,500 field pieces ranging in size from 3 to 18in in calibre. In addition, there were mobile gun platforms – tanks – and thousands of aircraft to help direct artillery barrage or direct bomb enemy targets.

Initially, in preparation for big battles the British used their artillery in massive barrages for days on end with the intention of destroying German defences ready for the Big Push. On the day itself troops would advance behind a wall of artillery fire – a moving barrage, which would knock out any remaining enemy positions. This was the theory at least. In practice, although the

A well-built and dry German trench. By contrast British trenches were rarely as well constructed. (Author)

preparatory barrages were terrible, the Germans were generally well dug-in and they gave very effective notice of a forthcoming British attack. In addition, particularly around Ypres, the barrages destroyed draining trenches and turned the battlefields into evil-smelling and cloying mud. And lastly because there was almost no communication between the advancing troops and the artillery providing the moving barrage support, so it was all too easy for artillery to shell the advancing troops or fail to destroy machine-gun nests and the like. New tactics of shorter, more concentrated bursts with greater support of the advancing troops were introduced, initially at the Battle of Messines in June 1917, but progressively along the whole of the Western Front during 1918.

The Germans too effectively used their artillery to destroy British positions and make life difficult for men in the front line and those coming to relieve them. At about dusk the Germans would often launch a fifteen-minute barrage, known to the British as the 'Hate'. In turn this might lead to an Allied response.

The Royal Regiment of Artillery comprised three elements:

- The Royal Horse Artillery: armed with light, mobile, horse-drawn guns that in theory provided firepower in support of the cavalry. But in the immobile conditions of the Western Front they increasingly supported the Royal Field Artillery;
- The Royal Field Artillery: the most numerous arm of the artillery, it was responsible for the medium-calibre guns and howitzers deployed close to the front line;
- The Royal Garrison Artillery: developed from fortress-based artillery located on British coasts. It was armed with heavy, large-calibre guns and howitzers with immense destructive power.

Royal Artillery units, usually called brigades, were responsible to brigade, divisional and corps CRAs, that is Commanders Royal Artillery.

A horse-drawn ambulance at Ypres, 1917. The ambulance would have been used to carry wounded men from Advance Dressing Stations to the Casualty Clearing Stations behind the front line. (Wellcome Images (Ref L0023337))

Less well known is the Royal Engineers, which had a large number of different specialisms, such as transportation (for example, building and maintaining the maze of narrow gauge railways which carried supplies up to the front), tunnelling under enemy lines and laying and exploding mines, surveying and preparing trench maps, chemical warfare, designing and preparing camouflage and even running the postal service. This last was undoubtedly the most appreciated by the men at the front!

The Royal Army Medical Corps (RAMC) was responsible for the medical care and also the provision of decent sanitation. A man's chances of survival depended on how quickly his wound was treated. The whole process was designed to achieve this as efficiently as possible.

Regimental Aid Post (RAP)

Closest to the front line was the Regimental Aid Post (RAP) run by the Battalion Medical Officer helped by the battalion orderlies and stretcher-bearers. The Medical Officer (MO) was embedded in the battalion and came from the Royal Army Medical Corps (RAMC). There was also a Sergeant or Corporal and perhaps one or two other ranks from the Corps as well. The quality of MOs varied tremendously, some were excellent while others were so poor that soldiers avoided seeing them unless they absolutely had to. The MO was also responsible for public health and ensuring the sanitation met the required standards. This was important if often overlooked work, but it ensured that there were few outbreaks of malaria, dysentery or enteric fever, which had debilitated so many men in previous wars.

In action, the RAP was situated a few yards behind the front line. The RMO was helped by the Regimental Stretcher-Bearers who traditionally were the regimental bandsmen.

The facilities were only sufficient to administer first aid. The object of the exercise was to patch up the casualties and either return them to their duties in the line or pass them back to an Advance Dressing Station (ADS).

In battle a casualty was to be transported direct to the ADS, but to avoid congestion Collecting Posts (CPs) and Relay Posts (RPs) were sometimes set up. This meant there were teams of RAMC stretcher-bearers strung out over miles of ground unpassable by motor or horsed transport, shuttling between the posts and passing the wounded on to the next team. A 'carry' could be anything up to 4 miles over muddy or shell-pocked ground, either in trenches or above ground.

Field Ambulance (Fd Amb or FA)

There was at least one but normally two ADSs set up by the Field Ambulances (Fd Amb or FA). Ideally, the Advance Dressing Station would be sited about 400yd behind the RAPs, in tents where necessary, but preferable in large houses or schools, with the Main Dressing Stations (MDS) sited a mile or so further back.

The FA was the most forward of the RAMC units. Each brigade had a FA assigned to it. When the brigade was out of the line the units were allocated special tasks such providing a centre for scabies or for other ailments, a Divisional Rest Centre (DRS) or as a bath unit.

An Infantry Field Ambulance comprised 10 officers and 182 other ranks from the RAMC. In each FA there was a Headquarters Company (A Section) which made up the Main Dressing Station and two Sections (B and C Coy) which formed the two ADSs. Each section was further sub-divided into the 'tent division', which comprised the medical staff and formed the treatment area, and the 'bearers', who collected the casualties from the RAPs, carried them back to the 'tent division' at the ADS or manned the relay posts.

The ADS was meant to provide sufficient treatment so men could be quickly returned to their units where possible. If the casualty was seriously wounded, he was sent to the Casualty Clearing Station (CCS). Later in the war fully equipped surgical teams were attached to the FAs.

Casualty Clearing Station (CCS)

The Casualty Clearing Stations (CCSs) facilitated movement of casualties from the battlefield on to the hospitals. They were very large units, with a minimum of 50 beds and 150 stretchers in order to treat a minimum of 200 sick and wounded at any one time. In normal circumstances the team would be made up of seven Medical Officers, one Quartermaster and seventy-seven other ranks, there would also be a Dentist, a Pathologist, seven nurses and other non-medical personnel including VADs.

They were usually situated about 12 miles (20km) behind the front lines; roughly mid-way between the front line and the Base Area, and about 500yd from a main railway line or waterway system. This was the first line of surgery and as close as the nursing staff would get to the front line. Even so, treatment was still only limited.

CCSs collected casualties from the ADSs by using Motor Ambulance Convoy. Each ambulance had an ASC driver and an RAMC attendant. The wounded would stay up to four weeks in order to recover before they returned to their units or were transferred by Ambulance Trains or Inland Water Transport to a hospital. The limited medical aid available meant that many men died, which is why the locations of many CCSs are marked by cemeteries.

Stationary Hospital/General Hospital/Base Area
There were two Stationary Hospitals to every Division and each one was designed to hold up to 400 casualties. There was, however, a tendency to use these as specialist hospitals, for example, sick, VD, gas victims, neurasthenia cases, epidemics, etc. They normally occupied what had been a civilian hospital.

A General Hospital was located on or near railway lines to facilitate movement of casualties from the CCSs on to the ports. Hotels and other large buildings such as casinos were requisitioned but some hospitals were hutted and constructed on open ground. In Base Areas such as Étaples and Boulogne General Hospitals had all the facilities of a normal civilian hospital. Men would be stay until they were either fully fit or they were sent back to Britain for specialist care or to recuperate from their wounds.

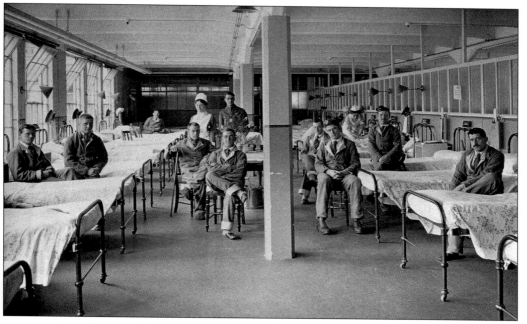

A ward in the King George Hospital, Stamford Street, London SE1. This hospital treated badly wounded ordinary soldiers. (The RAMC Muniment Collection in the care of the Wellcome Library)

The above section is based on the web page Chain of Evacuation on the RAMC website, www.ramc-ww1.com/chain _of_evacuation.php. More about the care of the wounded can be found, with lists of where many of the hospitals were based, at www.1914-1918.net/wounded.htm.

Despite the arrival of the lorry, the tank and the aeroplane, the First World War was not a heavily mechanised war. There was a constant demand for labour, to move stores and ammunition, mend roads and build dugouts.

For more details see the relevant pages on the Long, Long Trail and Western Front Association websites.

Units
Orders of Battle
Orders of battle (often referred to as Orbats) offer a guide to the British Army based on its structure. They can be of value because they list under which division, corps or army a battalion or unit served on and when they moved between the higher echelons. What you won't find, however, is the physical location of individual units. Orders are explained in more detail at www.greatwar.co.uk/research/military-records/ww1-orders-of-battle.htm.

During the 1930s the War Office published a series of volumes of orders of battle, as part of the series of Official Histories of the war, by Major A. F. Becke:

History of the Great War based on official documents by direction of the Historical Section of the Committee of Imperial Defence. Order of Battle of Divisions Part I: The Regular British Divisions, London, 1935

History of the Great War based on official documents by direction of the Historical Section of the Committee of Imperial Defence. Order of Battle of Divisions Part 2A: The Territorial Force Mounted Divisions and the 1st-Line Territorial Force Divisions (42–56), London, 1936

History of the Great War based on official documents by direction of the Historical Section of the Committee of Imperial Defence. Order of Battle of Divisions Part 2B: The 2nd-Line Territorial Force Divisions (57th–69th) with the Home Service Divisions (71st–73rd) and 74th and 75th Divisions, London, 1937

History of the Great War based on official documents by direction of the Historical Section of the Committee of Imperial Defence. Order of Battle of Divisions Part 3A: New Army Divisions (9–26), London, 1938

History of the Great War based on official documents by direction of the Historical Section of the Committee of Imperial Defence. Order

of Battle of Divisions Part 3B: New Army Divisions (30–41) and 63rd (R.N.) Division, London, 1945
History of the Great War based on official documents by direction of the Historical Section of the Committee of Imperial Defence. Order of Battle. Part 4 The Army Council, G.H.Q.s, Armies, and Corps, 1914–1918, London, 1945

These volumes give details of every division with its component brigades, battalions, artillery, engineers, medical support, etc., units and record any changes. There are also organisational tables for divisions in the various theatres of war. Included are the names of General Officers Commanding and brigade commanders and senior staff officers. Each division has a brief history listing the operations and battles in which it was engaged and the corps to which it was subordinated at the time. They were reprinted by the Naval & Military Press, but only Part 1 appears now still to be in print.

Perhaps easier to use are these books by Ray Westlake:

British Battalions on the Western Front, Pen & Sword, 2000; for the period between January and June 1915
British Battalions in France and Belgium, 1914, Pen & Sword, 1997

TNA also has sets of orders of battle in pieces WO 95/5467–5471.

However, you probably do not need to go down these somewhat tedious routes. Chris Baker's excellent Long, Long Trail website contains increasing numbers of orders of battle arranged by echelon or by unit.

Another useful shortcut is to look at the description of the Battalion or Unit War Diary to be found in the piece description on the Discovery catalogue on TNA's website. This will give you the brigade and division that the battalion or unit served with.

Official Histories

During the 1920s the government commissioned teams of historians to prepare detailed Official Histories of the war, formally known as the History of the Great War based on Official Documents. The intention was to learn lessons, both tactical and logistic, from the war and also to provide an authoritative historical account. Historians have often dismissed them as being mere propaganda – 'official but not history' in the military historian Basil Liddell Hart's tart phrase. But they are worth consulting, if for no other reason that they contain superb series of maps of the battlefields. However, they are likely to be hard going for the novice, as the Official Histories can be quite technical.

There are separate multi-volume series for each year on the Western Front which are listed on the Long, Long Trail website, www.1914-1918.net/official.html, and the Great War website, www.greatwar.co.uk/research/books/ww1-official-history.htm. Many reference libraries have incomplete sets. Between them the IWM and the Naval & Military Press have reprinted many volumes.

Before the histories were published drafts were sent to officers who had fought in the campaign for their comments. Their replies can be very informative and offer honest insights into how battles were viewed by officers, although often containing more than a hint of hindsight. Major Herbert Christie, who commanded the 12 Field Battery in the desperate days of October 1914:

> [on the 20th], the 12th was in action just behind the village of Kreuseike, we fired 'sending fire' over the Grenadiers (dug in just in front of the village) and I observed from a horse, our fuses burst beautifully, which speaks well for the Battery as it was a very dark night, and I kept the bursts low purposely.

[It] was [also] the day the enemy overran our trenches south of Kreuseike I took a section to the extreme south of the village, in response to an urgent call for help from the Border Regt and only returned [from] them just in time to avoid capture (we lost one gun team shot to pieces). We were at 'gun fire' for quite five minutes. The same afternoon I sent a section under Lt Woodhouse to support the Gordons, nearer Zandvoorde in response to a similar appeal. Both sections I believe materially delayed the attack. My gun pits behind Kreuseike were completely destroyed by shell fire that morning, a few moments after I had withdrawn the remaining gun (one was out of action from spring trouble). On the following morning Lt Woodhouse's section again moved to the support of the Gordons and I was told did excellent work.

Our casualties alone prove that we did our best at Ypres in 14 and fought right up in the front line. I lost two subalterns and my BQSM [Battery Quarter Sergeant Major] killed and I was shot myself and out of action until July 15. [WO 95/1643 and CAB 45/241]

The correspondence, together with a small collection of private diaries and related paperwork, including several enemy accounts, is at TNA in series CAB 45/215–261. You may also come across copies in the war diaries themselves, as with Major Christie.

Regimental Histories

Any regiment worth its name will have had several histories written about it. The first were published in the mid-nineteenth century and are still being written today. Between the wars, most regiments and service corps published specific histories relating to the unit during the Great War. Inevitably, they vary greatly in quality and interest. The best include interviews with former officers or copies of letters they wrote home describing incidents and battles. But most have a workmanlike approach providing an overview of what each battalion did theatre by theatre month by month. Although they are now rather dated, serious researchers should not ignore them.

Also worth looking out for are the divisional histories, which describe the war from the perspective of the division HQ.

There is a detailed bibliography arranged by regiment and arm available on the Army Museums Ogilby Trust website at www.armymuseums.org.uk. More complete are probably Roger Perkins, *Regiments: Regiments and Corps of the British Empire and Commonwealth 1758-1993: a Critical Bibliography of their Published Histories* (David & Charles, 1994) and Arthur S. White, *A Bibliography of Regimental Histories of the British Army* (Stamp Exchange, 1988).

The IWM and National Army Museum have major collections and TNA's library and the Society of Genealogists also have good collections. Regimental museums and local libraries should have those for units raised in their area. And many have been republished in facsimile form by the Naval & Military Press.

Since the 1970s there has been an explosion of unofficial battalion histories, such as the series about the Pals battalions for Pen & Sword, describing the activities of individual units. Most are meticulously researched and illustrated and are well worth looking out for.

Minor Sources

Regimental Magazines
By the 1920s almost every regiment published a quarterly magazine which contained many stories about regimental activities and listed promotions, the award of education certificates, cups for marksmanship and the minutiae of everyday life in the Army which on the whole was not recorded elsewhere.

In Flanders Fields

—

In Flanders fields the poppies blow
Between the crosses, row on row,
That mark our place; and in the sky
The larks, still bravely singing, fly
Scarce heard amid the guns below.

We are the Dead. Short days ago
We lived, felt dawn, saw sunset glow,
Loved, and were loved, and now we lie
          In Flanders fields.

Take up our quarrel with the foe:
To you from failing hands we throw
   The torch; be yours to hold it high.
   If ye break faith with us who die
We shall not sleep, though poppies grow
          In Flanders fields

Punch
Dec 8·1915   John McCrae
                                                —

A copy of John McCrae's famous poem 'In Flanders Fields'. (Author)

You might well find obituaries of old soldiers and memoirs of particular battles or actions experienced by the writer.

There is no national collection of these magazines, although the National Army Museum and the IWM have incomplete sets. The best place to look is in regimental archives. The Royal Logistics Corps has published online those for its 'forming corps', notably the Army Service Corps and Army Ordnance Corps. Details can be found at www.rlcarchive.org. Miles Templer (www.templer.net) has published a small selection on CD.

Soldiers Died in the Great War

Records relating to individual casualties are available on Ancestry and Findmypast (see Chapter 3). However, it is perfectly possible to manipulate this database to produce lists of men from particular units or towns. To do this you need to obtain a copy of Soldiers Died on CD from Naval & Military Press (for more details visit www.great-war-casualties.com). Alternatively, some local libraries, family history society research centres and Western Front Association branches may have the CD.

Chapter 11

RESEARCHING ACTIONS

Unit War Diaries

War diaries are the most important source in researching activities by Army units whether they were in the front line or stationed a long way from the action.

War diaries were introduced in 1908 and are still kept by units in action today. The diaries were designed to record unit activities, particularly when it was in action. This, it was felt, would help analysis by historians and strategists so that they could learn lessons for future wars: they are very much the first draft of history. They were kept by infantry battalions and artillery batteries as well as by higher echelons, such as brigades, divisions and even armies, as well as by more specialist units such as mobile hospitals, signals companies and field bakeries. With few exceptions they only survive for units that served outside Britain and Ireland.

For researchers they are the raw material of history because they contain the immediate records of each day's activities generally unfiltered by further reflection and occasionally contain the thoughts and feelings of the men compiling them. But naturally they are only concerned with the occurrences in their unit. To get the best from them you need to use the diaries in conjunction with other records, such as published histories, memoirs and diaries, and official histories. It is a shame that they have not been more used by popular historians, but perhaps this will change once they are all online.

War diaries were generally completed either by the commanding officer or in larger units by the adjutant who otherwise was responsible for the general administration of the unit. Inevitably, war diaries reflect the enthusiasm that the officer compiling the war diary had for the task, but most are reasonably detailed, particularly when the unit was in the front line.

It is very unusual to find individual privates and non-commissioned officers mentioned, unless they had received an immediate gallantry award, and even then they might not warrant

A page from the war diary for 7/8 Royal Irish Fusiliers for 7 June 1917, the first day of the Battle of Messines. War diaries are the most important source for studying exactly what happened day-by-day to each unit. (The National Archives WO 95/1978)

an entry. However, officers are generally mentioned, particularly when they are killed, wounded or less often when have been awarded gallantry medals, sent out to lead a patrol into no-man's-land, returned from leave or left on a training course.

As well as the diaries themselves there may be accompanying appendices. These might consist of regimental orders, plans of attack, maps and other ephemeral information, including on occasion lists of officers and men awarded gallantry medals. Of particular interest are typewritten operational reports, which supplement entries in the war diaries themselves.

It is important to remember that diaries were compiled by the battalion headquarters. Companies or sections may actually be based some way away from the headquarters and their experience can be very different to that of the centre and yet this may not be recorded. To an extent this is excusable by the heat and chaos of battle. If you are lucky you may be able to overcome this problem by using private papers, such as diaries, letters and memoirs.

Curiously, it is often difficult to know exactly where a battalion or unit was based. You may need a decent map of the area to be able to pick up the village where they were stationed behind the line – a modern road atlas should be fine. If a map reference is given then you should be able to find it on the appropriate trench map (see below).

War Diaries: Higher Echelons

In addition there are war diaries for brigades, divisions and higher echelons. Inevitably, these contain less about day-to-day activities on the front and more about planning battles and trench raids and meeting the logistical demands of tens of thousands of men.

However, I have found copies of reports that are no longer with the battalion records. Certainly it is worth checking the brigade diaries as well as the battalion ones as these can give an overview of what was actually going on in the trenches that a

Battalion War Diary cannot. In particular, you may find recommendations for the award of gallantry medals.

In fact, for the higher echelons war diaries are rather a misnomer. The actual war diary is often no more than a page or two per month and may just record the visit of senior officers and other inconsequential matters. The real meat lies in the accompanying appendices, which can include orders, reports, plans, maps and occasionally photographs. There will be much material about planning and preparation for battle, which question the myth that the men in the front line were not equipped for trench warfare. The appendices are doubly important because so much about how the war was planned or organised was destroyed in the disastrous fire at the Army Record Stores in Southwark in September 1940.

There should be war diaries for each component part of divisions, corps and armies, that is, general staff (responsible for the planning for and direction of the fighting), adjutant and quarter master general (administration and supplying troops in the field), artillery, engineers and medical, as well as those infantry and cavalry units which were attached to headquarters.

War Diaries: Location and Use

An almost complete set of diaries is at TNA is in series WO 95 (with a few 'confidential war diaries' in WO 154, which generally mention individuals who appeared before courts martial). They are arranged by army, corps, division and brigade, although in practice this doesn't matter because it is easy to pick up individual units through the Discovery catalogue. The diaries are arranged by month and consist of entries in pencil on loose sheets of paper. Appendices tend to be typed or in the form of cyclostyle copies.

TNA has digitised the diaries for units which served in France and Flanders only. It costs £3.30 to download a war diary, although you can still visit Kew to read them for yourself on one of the computers in the reading rooms. If a war diary has been digitised then the original is no longer available for researchers to use. This is amazing value for money, but there is one major disadvantage. Unless you have superfast broadband it can take hours to download diaries because individual files are generally massive.

However, there is an alternative in the form of the Naval and Military Archive (www.nmaarchive.com). At the time of writing only about half of the war diaries are available, but this will no doubt have changed by the time you read this. Instead of downloading the whole diary you can read war diaries page by page, which is fine if you want to find out about a particular 'stunt' or see whether there is anything about an individual casualty. The quality of the images is top notch, although the site itself is not terribly user friendly.

Despite all the evidence to the contrary, TNA does not have a complete set of diaries, so if the unit diary appears to be missing it is worth approaching the regimental archives as they often have duplicate copies. This is particularly the case with the Royal Artillery as TNA's holdings for the Artillery are rather patchy.

A few regimental museums have transcribed their sets of war diaries and put them online, generally free of charge. For example, the Wardrobe Museum in Salisbury, which is the regimental museum for the Berkshire and Wiltshire regiments, has put up the Battalion War Diaries for both world wars.

Official Despatches

After each war or campaign commanders-in-chief are expected to summarise the successes and failures in a despatch that is then published in the *London Gazette*. The ones for the First World War are surprisingly readable. In his final despatch, published in 1919, Haig used the services of the writer John Buchan and Sir Ian Hamilton, who commanded British forces for most of the

Gallipoli campaign and was a fluent and engaging author.

In it they traditionally mention service personnel of all ranks worthy of special praise, hence the term Mention in Despatches. They are now rarely used by historians, but might be of interest particularly if your ancestor was one of the thousands of men and women who were so Mentioned. It is rare, however, to find out why an individual was so commemorated.

The despatches are available online through the *London Gazette* (www.thegazette.co.uk), but it is probably easier to read the text on the Long, Long Trail website, although Chris Baker does not include any of the lists of names which accompanied the original despatches.

Photographs and Film

The largest collection by far of First World War related material is at the IWM. At the heart of the Museum's collections are 40,000 official photographs showing all aspects of the war. As it took time for a satisfactory system to be set up, and particularly to overcome suspicion from the military authorities, the photographic record is more comprehensive from mid-1916 onwards than for the first half of the war. Initially, a number of soldiers took cameras with them to the battlefields, but they were banned in the spring of 1915.

This collection is supplemented by material donated by individual servicemen. Many images, but certainly not all, are described in the online catalogue at www.iwm.org.uk/collections /search.

Regimental Museums and local studies libraries should also have collections of material. The Honourable Artillery Company archive, for example, has many photographs of soldiers who fell during the war, because the Company's secretary of the day wrote to the deceased's families asking for photographs.

The IWM's Film and Video Archive also has by far the largest

A British officer modelling an early gas mask. After their initial use by the Germans in April 1915, gas did not prove to be a decisive weapon in the war. This was because all men were issued with efficient gas respirators and were given anti-gas training. (Author)

collection of films. Its collection is described in Roger Smithers (ed.), *The Imperial War Museum Film Catalogue Volume 1: The First World War* (Flick Books, 1997).

The best-known film of the period is *The Battle of the Somme*, which was seen by two-thirds of the British population on its release in late 1916. It is now available on YouTube, or on DVD, and is worth watching as it offers a unique picture of the British Army on the Western Front.

There are also a number of regional film archives which may also have film of the period. The largest of these is the North West Film and Video Archive in Manchester.

Also worth checking out are newsreels – short news stories shown at local cinemas. Those for the First World War largely concentrate on the 'home front'. There is a list at http://bufvc.ac.uk/newsonscreen/search. British Pathe (www. britishpathe.com) and Movietone (www.movietone.com) have clips from the newsreels they made available on their websites free of charge. It is also well worth visiting YouTube as many films, including short documentaries and original films, have been put up there.

Trench Maps

From early 1915 British surveyors and mapmakers began to map the trenches using sketches drawn by observers in aircraft flying perilously along the Western Front.

The trenches were originally mapped at a scale of 1:10,000, that is roughly 6in to the mile, red lines (for German trenches) and blue (British; the colours however were reversed in 1918) are superimposed on a ghostly backdrop of the villages, woods and railways found on pre-war maps of Flanders and France, upon which these maps were based. Ammunition dumps, hospitals and other facilities reveal how far the countryside for miles behind the front line was appropriated by the military. And close to the front line the maps show the intricacies of the trench systems indicating individual command posts, machine guns, field batteries and so on, all plotted from air photographs.

The maps are very detailed, although it has to be said that they can be difficult to use. They will be of most use to people with considerable knowledge of the terrain.

Major collections of maps are held by both TNA (series WO

153 and WO 297) and the IWM. Local regimental museums and other archives may also have smaller collections.

Many maps, but certainly not all, have been scanned by McMaster University in Canada and can be viewed at http://library.mcmaster.ca/maps/ww1/ndx5to40.htm.

You can buy facsimiles in several ways. Paper copies of selected maps have been published by G. H. Smith and Son (www. ghsmithbookshop.com).

Otherwise sets are available on CD. The best such collection is undoubtedly *The National Archives British Trench Map Atlas* from Naval & Military Press (www.great-war-trench-maps.com /watm.htm), with hundreds of different maps in various editions. The Western Front Association has also published a small collection for the major battle zones.

Great War Digital (www.greatwardigital.com) is a company selling digitised trench maps which can be used in GPS systems. They are probably of greatest use when touring the battlefields.

Further Reading

The best introduction to these maps and how to use them is at www.greatwar.co.uk/research/maps/british-army-ww1-trench-maps.htm. In particular it contains a useful guide to interpreting map references that you might find in a war diary. Also useful is Chris Baker's explanation at www.1914-1918.net/trench_maps.htm. The best book is Peter Chasseaud, *Topography of Armageddon: a British trench map atlas of the Western Front, 1914–1918* (Mapbooks, 1991). Also of interest is Peter Chasseaud, *Artillery's Astrologers – A History of British Field Survey and Mapping on the Western Front, 1914–1918* (Mapbooks, 1999), and *Mapping the First World War: The Great War through maps from 1914–1918* (Imperial War Museum, 2013).

Chapter 12

THE WAR IN THE AIR

The Royal Air Force (RAF) is by far the youngest of the services, having been formed as late as 1 April 1918. It was a marriage of the Royal Flying Corps (RFC) and the Royal Naval Air Service (RNAS)

The First World War saw a rapid expansion in the air services and the work undertaken by aircraft. The RFC spent much of its time offering support to the Army on the Western Front and elsewhere by initially operating reconnaissance missions, and later through artillery spotting, and bombing German targets in Belgium. Until February 1916 the RNAS was responsible for the air defence of Britain (when it was transferred to the RFC), and was the pioneer of strategic bombing against Germany and sites in occupied Belgium from its base in Dunkirk. In addition, the service operated patrols from coastal air stations in Britain and from ships.

The mobility and freedom of the air was often contrasted with the stalemate of the trenches. Even so, the life of pilots and observers was usually merry and often short. In 1917 the life expectancy of a pilot on the Western Front was between eleven days and three weeks. That is if they survived the brutal period of training. Of the 14,000 pilots and aircrew in the RFC who were killed, well over half lost their lives in training.

There are several resources that cover the RAF as well as the other services. The *London Gazette* records the promotion and, to a degree, postings of officers as well as the award of gallantry medals. The Commonwealth War Graves Commission records the deaths of RAF personnel. In particular, the Flying Services Memorial in the Faubourg D'Arras Cemetery in Northern France commemorates nearly 1,000 airmen who have no known grave.

For men who served before the creation of the RAF in April 1918 you should also check the sources for the Army (RFC) and the Navy (RNAS).

There are Medal Index Cards for nearly 27,000 officers and airmen who transferred from the RFC to the RAF in April 1918. Where there is no card, exactly the same information can be found on the service records of airmen (but not on officers' records).

It can be difficult to find information about gallantry awards made to RFC, RNAS and RAF personnel. They are gazetted in the *London Gazette* (www.thegazette.co.uk), but rarely contain citations. There are, however, a few unindexed files containing citations which were presented to the King for his formal approval in series AIR 2 (code 30). Details of awards to RNAS personnel are available in Ancestry's naval medals collection.

Reports of aircraft (and pilot) casualties on the Western Front between March 1916 and April 1919 are in AIR 1/843–860, 865 with other lists in AIR 1/914–916, 960–969. The RAF Museum holds an extensive set of record cards relating to deaths, injuries and illness suffered by RFC and RAF personnel. These are now online at www.rafmuseumstoryvault.org.uk.

Service Records

Officers

TNA has service records for RAF officers and airmen who were discharged before the early 1920s. They include details about next of kin, civilian occupation, units in which an individual served, appointments and promotions, and honours and medals awarded. In addition, comments may have been added by training officers about the individual's flying skills or (more likely) lack of them. The records are considerably more informative for pilots, navigators and observers than for the engineering staff or the administrators. The records are all online via TNA website and Findmypast.

For pilots it is worth looking at the Royal Aero Club Aviators' Certificates on Ancestry, which contains approximately 28,000 index cards and 34 photograph albums of aviators who were issued with their flying licences by the Royal Aero Club, mainly between 1910 and late 1915. The cards include name, date of birth, birthplace, nationality, rank or profession, date and place of certificate, and certificate number.

RNAS officers' records are in ADM 273. They are arranged by service number order, although there is an index available through Discovery. The records will give you details of which units he served with, next of kin and comments by superior officers about performance and conduct.

Information about the officers and ratings of the RNAS who died during the war are in series ADM 242 (and online through Findmypast).

On the formation of the RAF a new Air Force List was issued along the lines of the Army and Navy Lists with brief details of officers. These are available at https://archive.org. The one for April 1918 is available at www.rafmuseumstoryvault.org.uk.

The war service of many pilots, particularly those regarded as 'aces' (that is those who shot down five or more enemy aircraft) have been researched and published in books, such as C. F. Shores, N. L. R. Franks and R. Guest, *Above the Trenches. A Complete Record of the Fighter Aces and Units of the British Empire Air Forces, 1915–1920* (Grub Street, 1990, with a supplement in 2002), and for bomber crews their *Above the War Fronts: A Complete Record of the British Two-Seater Bomber Pilot and Observer Aces, the British Two-Seater Fighter Observer Aces, and the Belgian, Italian, Austro-Hungarian and Russian Fighter Aces 1914–1918* (Grub Street, 1997).

Other Ranks

Records of RAF other ranks are online through Findmypast. Apart from personal details, these records include dates of enlistment and discharge, promotions and units served with, brief notes of medical and disciplinary history, and dates of service overseas. Also, they contain the same information as the Medal Index Cards, so if there isn't an actual card for your man, this is a more than adequate alternative.

In addition, TNA has a muster roll of all other ranks compiled in early April 1918, which is also available on Findmypast and, free of charge, at www.rafmuseumstoryvault.org.uk.

Operational Records

There are several series of operational records for the RFC, RNAS and RAF. Most records are to be found in series AIR 1 at TNA. Of particular importance are the daily communiqués, which summarise the events of the previous 24 hours including details of dogfights with enemy aircraft, and the surviving records of the squadrons themselves. However, the latter are very patchy. If you are lucky you will find a records book, which describes what the squadron did day-by-day. There will be other material, particularly for the Independent Force, which was established to engage in long-range raids on German cities.

Also of interest are the combat reports compiled by pilots, although they should be treated with some caution, as pilots tended to claim planes that they had not shot down. This was inevitable in the heat of battle when several RAF aircraft might be engaged in a dogfight with an enemy plane. The reports are arranged by squadron and can be found in AIR 1, although some are missing.

In recent years there have been a number of squadron histories and websites dedicated to their history, which are well worth checking out.

A major source for First World War military aviation is the RAF Museum. Of particular interest is their Story Vault website at www.rafmuseumstoryvault.org.uk, which contains much about the war, including copies of casualty cards and the Air Force List for April 1918. More material will be added shortly. The Museum has many collections of private papers, photographs, books and other material, although it has to be said that their Navigator catalogue is not easy to navigate.

Some material, particularly collections of aerial photographs, can be found at the IWM. The IWM has some private papers for RAF personnel as well, including those of the aviation and naval artist Harold Wylie, who kept an informative (but hard to read) diary. A typical entry is for 25 April 1915, while he was with 4 Squadron:

> Early reconnaissance with Hawker. Canal bridge, Morrslede, Besslere, Terhand, Zaandvoord. Brought two Germans to action and chased them down. Met a third who gave us hell with a machine gun. He plastered the air with bullets five of which hit us. One striking my steel plate, ripped my cushion across, and then cut across the back of my chair knocking a big hole in the other side of the machine . . .

Further Reading
Foley, Michael, *Pioneers of Aerial Combat: Air Battles of the First World War*, Pen & Sword, 2013
Franks, Norman, *Great War Fighter Aces, 1914–1916*, Pen & Sword, 2014
O'Connor, Mike, *Airfields and Airmen of Ypres*, Pen & Sword, 2000
Tomaselli, Phil, *Tracing Your RAF Ancestors*, Pen & Sword, 2009

There seems to be no authoritative website devoted to British military aviation during the First World War, although both www.theaerodrome.com and www.wwiaviation.com may be able to help. Cross and Cockade International is a society devoted to researching the war in the air. You can find out more at www.crossandcockade.com (the website also includes a number of useful resources).

Chapter 13

WOMEN IN FLANDERS

As well as men thousands of British and Commonwealth women saw service in Flanders as nurses, clerks and engaged in other trades. However, as far as it is known, none went into the trenches, apart from the rather special case of Dorothy Lawrence who enlisted into the Royal Engineers as Sapper Dennis Smith.

Despite their contribution to the war effort, there are relatively few records for women. And before you start you have to have a rough idea at least about your ancestor's war service.

Many of the records for women are identical for their menfolk. In particular, women who served overseas either in the forces or as a volunteer in a hospital or canteen were entitled to the same campaign medals as men. Details of these awards can be found in the Medal Index Cards (and Medal Rolls) in the same way you would research a soldier or sailor. The information given is identical, although it is generally not terribly helpful. However, Ancestry's set does not include women recipients so you must use those on TNA's website.

The appointment, promotion and resignation of officers in the nursing services and auxiliary corps should be recorded in the *London Gazette*. In addition, the *Gazette* lists the award of gallantry medals to women (generally the Royal Red Cross and mentions in despatches).

Several thousand women were killed on active service. They are commemorated in the normal way by the Commonwealth War Graves Commission. In addition, many Army workers, nurses and VADs are listed in Soldiers Died in Great War, including some who died in Britain.

Nurses

By the middle of 1917 some 45,000 nurses were serving in the armed forces and thousands more women were doing auxiliary work in hospitals at home and in France. Before the war Queen Alexandra's Imperial Military Nursing Service (QAIMNS) had maintained small nursing services, which greatly expanded during the war.

Service records for Army nurses, including members of the Territorial Force Nursing Service, are online on TNA's website. The records can tell you where a nurse trained, references relating to their suitability as military nurses, which hospitals, Field Ambulances, Casualty Clearing Stations or other medical units they served in, confidential reports about their performance, and when they left the services.

Nurses could be awarded the Royal Red Cross for meritorious service. The Royal Red Cross was created in 1883 by Queen Victoria, as an award to nursing sisters or ladies for outstanding service in the care of the sick or wounded of the armed services. Just over 6,700 awards were made during the war, but too often to administrators rather than nurses near the front.

This decoration had two classes, first class (members) with the post nominal letters RRC and second class (associates) ARRC. Awards were announced in the *London Gazette* and there are registers in series WO 145, but they may not tell you anything you haven't already gleaned from the *London Gazette*, except the dignatory who presented the medal, where and the date it happened. Using the information it may be worth seeing whether there was a story published in the local newspaper about the presentation.

Findmypast has a small database of military nurses who were

active in the early twentieth century, including some 1,600 volunteers who served with the Scottish Women's Hospital.

Voluntary Aid Detachments (VADs)

The British Red Cross Society and the Order of St John had in 1909 set up a nationwide network of Voluntary Aid Detachments (VAD). These were made up of men and women who would help in hospitals and provide other assistance on the outbreak of war. These people became known as VADs.

The nursing assistants – VADs – had a mixed reputation. In general they were badly treated by nurses and doctors, when not ignored altogether. Edie Appelton, an experienced Army nurse, wrote in her diary for 29 November 1915, that:

> The V.A.D.s are a source of great interest to me – taking them as a bunch they are splendid. They may be roughly divided into 4 sorts: 'Stalkers', 'Crawlers', the irresponsible butterflyers and the sturdy pushers.
>
> At the moment I am thinking of a butterfly one who is on night duty in these wards and says with a light hearted laugh: 'It's rippin' nursin' the men, great fun, when I was in the Officers' ward I did housework all the time, great fun – but there men are really ill – great fun.' When I show her how to do anything fresh, she twitches to get at it and says 'oh do let me try, I'd love to do that, simply love to.' She is an aristocratic little person most dainty and well groomed and the thought of her doing scrubbing and dusting all day – makes me smile. [www.edithappleton.org.uk]

VADs were members either of the British Red Cross Society or the Order of St John. Both organisations kept record cards for individuals, which may include the dates of service, the nature of the duties performed, the detachment the individual belonged to, the institutions and places where the individual served, and any honours that they may have been awarded. In addition, there are indexes for personnel who served in military hospitals, who were trained nurses and who received the campaign medals.

Unfortunately, neither set of cards is available to researchers at the time of writing, although the records are likely to be online by the time this book is published. Find out more at www. redcross.org.uk.

Further Reading
Sue Light's superb Scarlet Finders website www.scarletfinders. co.uk/index.html has lots about military nursing during the two world wars with an emphasis on the First. She also writes a fascinating blog on nurses of the First World War at http:// greatwarnurses.blogspot.com.

Auxiliary Corps

The Royal Navy in 1916 was the first service to recruit women to take over the roles of cooks, clerks, wireless telegraphists, code experts and electricians, although it was not until November 1917 that a separate Women's Royal Naval Service (WRNS) was set up. The Army noted the success of the Navy's experiment and rather nervously established the Women's Army Auxiliary Corps (WAAC, later Queen Mary's Army Auxiliary Corps (QMAAC)) in March 1917 to undertake similar work so releasing men for the front. There was widespread concern about morals, particularly if young men and young women worked in close proximity, and doubts about the ability of women to undertake the duties assigned them. All of these worries proved to be unfounded.

The WAAC was divided into four sections: Cookery; Mechanical; Clerical; and Miscellaneous. Most women stayed on the home front but around 9,000 served in France and Flanders.

The grades (ranks) were divided into Controllers and Administrators (officers) and Members (other ranks). Within the Members there were forewomen (sergeants), assistant forewomen (corporals) and workers (privates). And inevitably a member was still paid less than a man in the Army doing the same work. The WAAC uniform and accommodation were provided free but there was a weekly mess charge for food.

Only about 9,000 records survive for the 57,000 who served in the WAAC during the First World War. They do not include any for officials (aka officers), or the several hundred members who died while on active service. The records are surprisingly detailed with applications to join, references and correspondence about leaving, often to get married. However, there is very little about the member's service, although the Casualty Form will indicate which units she served with and may give details of period of leave or time spent in hospital. You may find mention of the Connaught Club, which was the headquarters of the Corps.

These records are online via TNA's website. An incomplete nominal roll for members of the Corps is in piece WO 162/16 at Kew with a list of women drivers employed during the war in WO 162/62. Recommendations for honours and awards are in WO 162/65. The war diaries are only for units that saw service in France and Flanders, but if your ancestor served overseas (and you know the unit) you may well find mention of her arrival or departure, particularly if she was an official.

WRAF

On the establishment of the RAF in April 1918 a separate Women's Royal Air Force (WRAF) was also set up, which was divided into four basic trades: Clerks and Storewomen; Household; Technical; and Non-Technical. Initially, little training was given and wages were based on existing experience and skills.

The majority of women were employed as clerks, with shorthand typists the most highly paid of all airwomen. Women allocated to the Household section worked the longest hours, doing back-breaking work for the lowest pay. The Technical section covered a wide range of trades, most highly skilled, including tinsmiths, fitters and welders.

The eight officials and seventy-five members who died as the result of enemy action can be found in the Soldiers of the Great War database. An extensive collection of material relating to the QMAAC is held in the Templar Study Centre at the National Army Museum in London (www.national-army-musuem.ac.uk), and includes photographs and personal papers (although no nominal rolls or service records).

Only records for other ranks in the WRAF survive and are to be found in series AIR 80. No records for officers are known to survive, but those for airwomen are available through TNA's website. They are uninformative, often consisting only of the certificate of discharge on demobilisation, of which each airwoman was given a copy. This gives service number, name, rank, air-force trade, date and place of enrolment and date and place of demobilisation. The Library at the RAF Museum (www.rafmuseum.org.uk) holds photographs of the WRAF at work, diaries, letters, typed accounts, badges, medals, certificates and other memorabilia.

Further Reading

Ingham, Mary, *Tracing Your First World War Service Women Ancestors*, Pen & Sword, 2012, offers an excellent guide to this surprisingly complicated subject.

Chapter 14

RESEARCHING THE DOMINION AND INDIAN TROOPS

The First World War was a war involving participants from many different nations. In particular, men, and a few women, from all four corners of the British Empire came to help the Mother Country.

When Britain declared war on 4 August 1914 she did so on behalf of the Empire as well as the United Kingdom itself. The five Dominions – Australia, Canada, Newfoundland, New Zealand and South Africa – were self-governing, but generally left their defence and foreign affairs to the British government. In part this reflected a belief in most people's minds that they were as British as any Londoner, Dubliner or Glaswegian. So it was natural that when the call came the Dominions would not be found wanting, although recent studies have found that a high proportion of the Canadian and Australian troops, in particular, had been born in Britain and so presumably had closer ties to the home country than did men who were born in the Colonies. And occasionally you may find British men who managed to enlist in the colonial forces because the pay was better and the discipline less irksome. But wherever they came from these 'colonial troops' were often regarded as being the crack troops of the British Army.

There was also the semi-autonomous Indian Empire based in New Delhi, which maintained the Indian Army, under the direct control of the Viceroy. The Army was largely led by British officers, with native troops as ordinary soldiers and non-commissioned

Indian regiments played a key part in the early months of the war. Khudadad Khan of 129th Duke of Connaught's Own Baluchis was the first Indian recipient of the Victoria Cross. On 31 October 1914, at Hollebeke, Belgium, the British officer in charge of the detachment having been wounded, and the other gun put out of action by a shell, Sepoy Khudadad, though himself wounded, remained working his gun until all the other five men of the gun detachment had been killed. (Author)

officers. Units from the Indian Army were rushed into the front line in the autumn and winter of 1914. By the spring of 1915 they were increasingly a rare sight around Ypres, because of a purely racist feeling that this was a white man's war.

There were also small numbers of other colonial troops in the front line, such as Rhodesians and Fijian planters. West Indians in particular were used as labourers.

In general the records are very similar to those you may be familiar with when researching British servicemen or British Army units. Indeed there are some shared records:

- The Commonwealth War Graves Commission records the last resting place of all Dominion and Indian troops;
- Gallantry awards for all ranks and the commissions and promotion of officers in Dominion forces appear in the *London Gazette*;
- War diaries of many units are at TNA in series WO 95.

Australia

The National Archives of Australia holds service documents for, among other formations, the 1st Australian Imperial Force (AIF), Australian Flying Corps, Australian Army Nursing Service and Depot or home records for personnel who served within Australia. The records are at www.naa.gov.au/collection/explore/defence/service-records/army-wwi.aspx. Also of interest is the AIF Project, which lists the details of those who served overseas with the Australian Imperial Force (www.aif.adfa.edu.au).

The Australian War Memorial (www.awm.gov.au) has a superb collection of material relating to Australian forces since 1901. Many records have been indexed or digitised, and placed online free of charge. You can find details at www.awm.gov.au/collection/digitised-record. The material includes:

- A roll of honour with some personnel details;
- First World War Embarkation Roll which contains details of approximately 330,000 AIF personnel as they left on overseas service;
- First World War Nominal Roll with details of 324,000 AIF personnel who served overseas;
- Honours and awards with details of recommendations made to members of the AIF;
- War diaries compiled by Australian units;
- Official Histories commissioned by the Australian government.

Through the Anzac Collections programme the Memorial is digitising the personal papers and diaries of 150 Anzacs. Details are at www.awm.gov.au/1914-1918/anzac-connections. Also available are the papers of General John Monash. By profession a civil engineer, he became one of the war's outstanding commanders. His papers give a comprehensive view of his wartime military career: from his command of the 4th Australian Brigade on Gallipoli to commanding the Australian Corps in 1918. Don't forget if you are ever in Canberra, the Australian War Memorial is definitely well worth visiting.

The National Library of Australia's Trove website (www.trove.nla.gov.au) is a brilliant resource with digitised newspapers, books, photographs and personal papers. As might be expected, there is a lot of material about the Western Front, including newspaper reports, contemporary books and photographs.

There are also a number of excellent websites devoted to the ANZACs. The Australian War Memorial (www.awm.org.au) has masses of information about the Australian (and to an extent New Zealand) involvement in France and Flanders, although it is not always easy to find. Official Histories prepared by both the Australian and New Zealand governments in the early 1920s can be downloaded from the Internet Archive website free of charge.

Canada

Library and Archives Canada holds many records for men and women who served in the Canadian forces during the First World War. A proportion of which are available online through the Collections Canada portal (www.collectionscanada.ca). Unfortunately, the databases are not always easy to use and the information, available partial. Before you start it might be worth looking at their First World War Search Topic, which explains what is available, at www.collectionscanada.gc.ca/genealogy/022-909.006-e.html.

Over 600,000 men and women enlisted in the Canadian Expeditionary Force (CEF) during the First World War (1914–18) as soldiers, nurses and chaplains. At the time of writing Library and Archives Canada (LAC) is digitising all their service files. They expect to complete the work during 2015. Unfortunately, the records have been heavily weeded, and only key documents survive.

Also available are the war diaries for Canadian units, all of which have long been digitised. You can find them at www. collectionscanada.gc.ca/archivianet/02015202_e.html. Copies of some war diaries are available at the UK National Archives at Kew.

The Canadian Virtual War Memorial, www.vac-acc.gc.ca/rem embers/sub.cfm?source=collections/virtualmem contains details of Canadians who died in the war and their last resting place. The information is similar to that available from the Commonwealth War Graves Commission. In addition, the website also has pages about Canada during the First World War. Possibly of more use are the Circumstances of Death files for individuals which are available at www.ancestry.ca (British subscribers will need to pay extra to use databases here), although unindexed records are available on the Collections Canada website.

Service records for members of the Royal Canadian Navy and Volunteer Reserve are with Library and Archives Canada. Also worth looking at are the Service Ledgers. Details of honours and awards to Canadian naval personnel can be found at www.rcnvr.com.

Further Reading
Wright, Glen, *Canadians at War 1914-1918: A Research Guide to War Service Records* (Global Genealogy Press, 2010)

New Zealand

Personnel records of 120,000 men who served in the New Zealand Expeditionary Force and were discharged before the end of 1920 are held by Archives New Zealand. They can be download at http://archway.archives.govt.nz, alt. In addition, the Archives has nominal and casualty rolls, rolls of honour, a few unit (war) diaries (the majority were destroyed in 1931) and records relating to honours and awards, which are briefly described in a research guide at http://archives.govt.nz/research/guides/war#first. Some regimental and official histories for New Zealand are available at http://nzetc.victoria.ac.nz/tm/scholarly/tei-corpus-WH1.html.

TNA has some war diaries for New Zealand units in series WO 95.

The Auckland War Memorial Museum's Cenotaph Database at http://muse.aucklandmuseum.com/databases/cenotaph has brief details about most New Zealand troops, particularly those who did not return. The Database is being redeveloped for the centenary.

The National Library of New Zealand has digitised many of the country's newspapers which are now available through the excellent Papers Past website (http://paperspast.natlib.govt.nz).

The Library also has a very good introductory leaflet explaining how to research the War with links to key resources and archives (http://natlib.govt.nz/researchers/guides/first-world-war), as well as to those of the Library's own collections that have already been digitised. This includes several collections of photographs.

India

The location of the service records of Indian privates and non-commissioned officers is not known. A few Medal Index Cards survive, generally for men who served in colonial campaigns that took place in 1918 and 1919. These are available on both TNA's website and Ancestry. The remainder of the cards are thought to have been destroyed.

Records for British officers in the Indian Army are at the British Library in London (www.bl.uk). Unfortunately, there are many different, and at times duplicating, sources, which can make research difficult.

Perhaps the best place to start is with an online database (http://indiafamily.bl.uk/UI) to British civil and military employees living in India, but it is by no means complete.

Service records for European officers and warrant officers are series IOL L/MIL/14. Some indexes are online at www.nationalarchives. gov.uk/a2a. However, it may be easier to use the British Library's own catalogue to its own Archives and Manuscripts at http: //searcharchives.bl.uk.

War diaries for many Indian units who served in Flanders are in series WO 95 at Kew.

Further Reading
Jolly, Emma, *Tracing Your British Indian Ancestors*, Pen & Sword, 2010

Newfoundland

Library and Archives Canada holds many records for men and women who served in the Canadian and Newfoundland forces during the First World War at Collections Canada portal (www.collectionscanada.ca). Unfortunately, the databases are not always easy to use and the information available partial, but there is help at www.collectionscanada.gc.ca/genealogy/022-909.006-e.html.

Surviving service records of the Newfoundland Regiment are online at www.therooms.ca/regiment/part3_database.asp. War diaries are at TNA in piece WO 95/ 4312. There's a website devoted to the history of the Regiment at www.rnfldr.ca/history.aspx?item=41.

South Africa

Service records are held by the South African National Defence Force, Documentation Service, Private Bag X289, Pretoria 0001, South Africa, email sandfdoc@mweb.co.za.

There is very little online about men who served in the South African forces during the First World War. One exception is the excellent website of the South African Military History Society at http://samilitaryhistory.org, which has much about the country's involvement in the First World War. It also provides details of the various military museums in South Africa.

Chapter 15

TOURISM

If you can, you really should get to the battlefields to see for yourself where the men fought. In some ways there is more to be found there and in some ways less than you might expect. The highlights undoubtedly are the immaculately kept Commonwealth War Graves Commission cemeteries and the museums.

Apart from a few German fortifications that proved impossible to demolish, the occasional shell hole which has become a farm pond and the very occasional strip of trench there are now very few reminders of the devastation that the war brought to the region. However, tons of shrapnel pieces, bullets and the odd shell are still found each year by farmers. If you visit in early spring you may see neatly stacked piles by the sides of roads waiting to be recovered by the local police. The Belgian Army is still decommissioning over 200 tonnes of these munitions every year. Tempting though it may be, you should not touch anything, because it can still kill or wound. In February 2014 two workmen were killed as they tried to move a shell found on a building site in Ypres.

When local farmers came back to their land in the 1920s they did their best to return it to what it was before the war. And over the decades they have largely succeeded. Just ten years after the Armistice, in 1928, H. A. Taylor wrote in a guidebook to the Western Front that those 'who visit the Messines battlefield with the object of locating those nineteen mine craters or the sites thereof, will spend much time and energy in vain for the Belgian farmer is not sentimental in his attitude to war relics. His one ambition is to obliterate them and to add to the cultivated area of his holding.'

In Ypres the British government fought a losing campaign against local residents. Initially, Winston Churchill, who was then Secretary of State for War, wanted to leave the whole of the town in ruins as a memorial to the sons of Empire who did not return home. But by 1920 the government had agreed with the Belgian authorities that only the Cathedral and the Cloth Hall, Ypres' most famous landmarks, were to remain in ruins. But the men and women who returned to their homes had no such sentiments and certainly did not want to be reminded of what they had had endured on a daily basis. Indeed, there almost no physical reminders left. By the late 1920s H. A. Taylor found that: 'every house is new; and yet the whole closely knit with very few gaps is pleasing to the eye. There is neither monotony nor obtrusiveness: every house holds your attention by reason of the craftsmanship shown in its brickwork.' And this remains true today, there is no sense that Ypres is not centuries old.

By the Second World War both the Cathedral and the Cloth Hall had been restored more or less to their pre-war glory. Instead, the Glorious Dead are commemorated at the Menin Gate, which is, in my view, a far more fitting and moving memorial.

Tourists have visited the battlefields since the Armistice. Even during the war itself the Army had to deal with influential sightseers. In 1917 and 1918 the *Guardian* journalist C. E. Montague, a wartime captain, took parties of journalists and guided guests, such as H. G. Wells and Bernard Shaw, along the Western Front. Among early visitors in 1919 and 1920 were the families who sought the last resting place of their beloved, sightseers who wanted to see the places they had read so much about and a surprising number of ex-servicemen wishing to revisit the places where they had fought. During the 1920s and

1930s the British Legion organised a number of 'pilgrimages' for ex-servicemen and their families, and in 1928 10,000 men took part.

It is surprisingly easy to get to Flanders from almost anywhere in Britain. During the war itself men going on leave were generally home within twenty-four hours of departing from the trenches. Today of course the journey takes a fraction of the time. You can fly to Brussels in an hour and then take a train to Ypres or hire a car. Eurostar trains speed to Lille and Brussels from where there are connecting trains to Ypres and Poperinge. Or you can take your car on a cross-Channel ferry or the Eurotunnel. Years ago I did a day trip to Ypres leaving London at about 6.30am and arriving in Ypres in time for a late breakfast.

And once you are in the Salient, the roads are good, or you can cycle between the sites or even walk (although the Belgian like their French neighbours still regard walkers with some bemusement). There's also a bus service connecting outlying villages with Ypres and Poperinge (details at www.delijn.be/en).

There are a reasonable number of hotels, and more have been built in recent years. In any case, perhaps, it might be best advised to try to stay out of season if possible, in part because it will be quieter, but also on a chilly windswept day with the threat of rain there's often a real sense of what it was actually like.

The centre of battlefield tourism in the Salient is, and always has been, Ypres. In 1928 H. A. Taylor said that:

> to this small square of territory comes more English speaking people than to any other part of the old battlefields. Never a day passes, winter or summer, but what a little group of people will be found examining the map of war graves which is hung on a little shelter among the ruins of the Cloth Hall, prior to setting off by car, or indeed on foot, along the road of remembrance which begins at the new Menin Gate and leads to a score of small

places whose names will ever be graven boldly in the history of British arms.

Initially, visitors slept in old Army huts and ate at temporary canteens and bars. As early as July 1919 a British resident, Lieutenant-Colonel Beckles Willson, complained to the Belgian Foreign Minister that 'the noble Grand Place [had been] vulgarised and desecrated by the erection of cheap and gaudily painted barraquements. . . . Even as I write six new huts are in the process of erection – all estaminets. One which is painted sky blue boldly calls itself "The British Tavern". . .'.

Now Ypres is a prosperous Flemish market town and wears its links to the First World War lightly, yet any visit is a moving experience. And despite the hordes of visitors, it is surprisingly untouristy. Unless things have changed recently, it is still remarkably hard to get a good meal or find a decent bar. If these things matter (and they do to me), then you might wish to stay in Poperinge.

It is possible to do a self-guided tour of the sites for yourself. The cemeteries in particular are well signposted. Details of a number of guidebooks are given below.

An alternative is to take a guided tour. Such tours have been available almost since the Armistice. Initially, they were often conducted by old soldiers, who for one reason or another, had not returned home. Alternatively, you could hire a car and a driver to take you out to the places you particularly wanted to visit. The Wipers Auto Service offered 'Private Touring Cars for Hire' and urged potential customers 'Don't waste your cash – come to us'. This was particularly appealing in the 1920s when the infrastructure was still being rebuilt. Travelling in a chauffeur driven car with a couple of friends, Major Charles Fair DSO of the 19th London Regiment revisited the Western Front in 1920. He wrote up the trip for his regimental magazine:

The last day of our tour was spent in such places as Boesinghe, St. Julien, Zillebeke, and last but not least The Bluff. Here I found the old tunnels, fallen in it is true, but still easily recognizable. I could stand at the entrance to battalion H.Q. and almost hear the voice of R.S.M. Trezona sending off ration parties. I am sure the Stretcher Bearers will grieve to know that there was some rubbish visible in some of the neighbouring shell holes! Then on up along the 'Wynd' we went, which, at the top, is apparently a natural pond, so no wonder we failed to drain it! At last we stood right on the top of 'A' crater and looked out on all sides at the scarred and battered country beyond. This was certainly one of the most impressive sights of all. The effects of war upon nature are shown here in all their hideousness, and while we stood there, to make a final scene to carry away in one's mind, some Belgian engineers exploded a dump of shells near Ypres with the dull familiar roar, without which the place would not have seemed real. [source: www.hellfirecorner.co.uk/cfair/haunts.htm]

Today there are a number of tour companies who will pick you up at your hotel and take you to see the main sites, or, if you ask, design a day or half-day tour to meet your specifications. One of the best, according to TripAdvisor, is Ypres 1914–18 Battlefield Tours (www.ypres-fbt.com), but of course there are other companies who offer similar services.

Another popular way of travelling to Flanders is with a guided tour, which includes travel from the UK, hotels meals and a guide. In 1919 Thomas Cook offered a deluxe tour for 35 guineas and a popular one for £9 9s. Today prices are rather higher. There are many companies that provide tours. Most offer general introductory tours, but it is possible to go on more specific trips perhaps to study a particular battle or the war poets. Here are five companies that regularly run tours, but no doubt there are others equally as good:

Battlefield Breaks – http://battlefield-breaks.com
Battle Honours – www.battle-honours.eu
Holts Tours – http://holts.co.uk
Leger Holidays – www.visitbattlefields.co.uk
Spirit of Remembrance – www.spiritofremembrance.com

In addition, the Western Front Association run several tours a year, and details can be found at www.westernfrontassociation. com/wfa-tours.html.

Or you can commission a bespoke tour, perhaps to visit the places where an ancestor served or looking at a specific action in greater detail. Matt Limb Battlefield Tours (www.mlbft.co.uk) is one such company. But again there are lots of alternatives.

To get full value you need to be sure that a member of the Guild of Battlefield Guides is leading the tour, as Guild members are extremely knowledgeable about the fighting and the area you are touring and are used to dealing with groups.

There is a surprising amount to do and see while you are in the Salient, and below is a list of key sites. The information includes addresses, opening days and so on, but it is wise to check before you go, just in case things have changed.

In addition, of course, there are nearly 200 CWGC cemeteries. These range from tiny ones in churchyards, like the one at Heestert where my Great-Uncle Stanley Crozier is buried, and small plots like the 'Aristocrat's Cemetery' at Zillebeke, where there are just thirty-two burials, many of them from noble families so hence the cemetery's name, to large graveyards where thousands of men lie. There are also many memorials to units and individuals, with just too many to list here. One of the finest memorials is 'the Brooding Soldier' at Vancouver Corner, Poelkappelle, which was erected to honour the Canadians of the 1st Canadian Division who were wiped out by one of the first gas attacks on 24 April 1915. The ferns in the little garden surrounding the monument are meant to mimic the creeping green-hewed gas. Or a memorial might take the form of a plaque on a building, such as the one on a cafe in Langemarck to the Irish poet Francis Ledwidge, who was killed on 31 July 1917 (and is buried in the Artillery Wood Cemetery).

Memorials are still being erected. As this book was finished, a new Red Dragon Memorial to the men from Wales who died around Ypres was unveiled on Pilckem Ridge by Carwyn Jones, the Welsh First Minister.

Details of all British and Commonwealth war graves are available through the Commonwealth War Graves Commission website www.cwgc.org. So far as I know there is no list of memorials online, but most will be described in the Holts' guide.

A display at the In Flanders Fields Museum at Ypres. (In Flanders Fields Museum)

Must-see Places

In Flanders Field Museum
Grote Markt 34
Ieper
www.inflandersfields.be
Open daily (not Mondays November–March and for most of January)
Admission charge

This is the best museum dedicated to the First World War in Belgium with a range of fascinating displays on all aspects of the war in Flanders, including the experiences of local people whose world was turned upside down by the events of 1914–18. It was reconfigured in 2012 in preparation for the centenary. In particular, you can now climb the bell tower with fine views all over what was the Salient. A nice touch is the use of poppy bracelets with imbedded RFID-chips that allow the wearer to read the stories of individual men and women from all sides at their own speed, as well as filmed monologues and aerial photography over the battlefields. The website contains a database listing casualties on both sides.

Langemarck German Cemetery
Langemarck
Open daily
Admission free

German cemeteries are sombre affairs reinforced by the use of dark stone. Langemarck Cemetery at the edge of Langemarck village is one of four German cemeteries in Flanders and the only one in the Ypres Salient. Over 44,000 men are buried here, most in mass graves. This sombre feeling is mirrored in four mourning figures at the rear of the graveyard. Visiting Langemarck graphically reinforces German losses.

Also worth visiting is the German cemetery at Vladso, near Dixmude. Here are two sculptures by Käthe Kollwitz called the 'Grieving Parents', which she made in memory of her only son, Peter, who was killed near Ypres on 22 October 1914.

Further Reading
Sheldon, Jack, *The German Army at Passchendaele*, Pen & Sword, 2014
Sheldon, Jack, *The German Army at Ypres*, Pen & Sword, 2010

Menin Gate
Mensestrrat
Ieper
www.cwgc.org
www.lastpost.be
Open daily
Admission free

The Menin Gate was dedicated in 1927 as the memorial to the missing from Britain and the Commonwealth who have no

A view of the Menin Gate showing a few of the 54,000 names of the missing to be found here. (In Flanders Fields Museum)

known grave. The site was chosen because of the hundreds of thousands of men who passed through it on their way to the battlefields. It was designed by Sir Robert Blomfield. There are 54,406 names inscribed on the walls. In fact, only men who were killed before 15 August 1917 appear here. The names of the 34,000 missing after this date are at Tyne Cot.

Each night promptly at 8pm a trumpeter from the local fire brigade sounds the 'Last Post'. Apart from the German occupation between May 1940 and September 1944, this simple and moving ceremony has been held every night since 1928. Nick Mansfield remembers when he went with his father and uncle in August 1964 'two men in dirty blue overalls (firemen I later gathered) rode up on their bicycles in the drizzle. They dismounted, drew out bugles from saddlebags and played a sad lament to us the only people present – which reverberated in the vast structure.' Now the ceremony is a key part of any tour to the Salient. The simple and extremely moving ceremony silences even the most boisterous school group. To get a place where you can see anything you need to be there by at least 7.30pm.

Further Reading
Dendooven, Dominiek, *Ypres as Holy Ground: Menin Gate and the Last Post*, de Klaproos, 2001

Talbot House
Gasthuisstraat 43
Poperinge
www.talbothouse.be
Open Tuesday–Sunday (Mondays are for group visits only)
Admission charge

Talbot House, Poperinge was opened in November 1915 as a 'Soldiers Club' – a haven from hell – by two chaplains of the 6th Division, Philip 'Tubby' Clayton and Neville Talbot. The house was dedicated to the memory of Gilbert Talbot, Neville's brother, who was killed in July 1915. For the following three years, except for a short period in 1918, the doors of Talbot House never closed and it became a 'home-from-home' for the officers and men of the British and Imperial armies of the time. Uniquely, it proclaimed itself as being an 'Every Man's Club' and soldiers were urged, 'All rank abandon ye who enter here'.

Surprisingly, Talbot House is still in existence and looking much as it did a century ago. There are few places in the Salient where there is such a direct link to the First World War and at times one almost senses the presence of the soldiers themselves. Incidentally, entries from the visitor's books have been digitised and are available through their website. It is also possible to stay at Talbot House.

Further Reading
Chapman, Paul and Ted Smith, *A Haven in Hell*, Pen & Sword, 2000

Tyne Cot Cemetery
Vijfwegestraat 5
Zonnebeke
www.cwgc.org.uk
Open daily (the visitor centre may be closed in December and January)
Admission free

This is the largest CWGC cemetery by numbers buried in the world and quite likely the most visited. There almost always seems to be a coach party or two walking among the graves or pondering the names on the memorial to the missing.

Tyne Cot, or Tyne Cottage, was the name given by the Northumberland Fusiliers to a barn which became the site of a network of German blockhouses, or pillboxes, the largest of which was used as an Advanced Dressing Station after its capture by Australian infantry in October 1917. Originally, nearly 350 men were buried here, but it was greatly enlarged after the Armistice when remains were brought in from smaller cemeteries or recovered from battlefields in the area.

The Cross of Sacrifice is placed on the largest of the pillboxes. From its steps you can clearly see Ypres, 5 miles away, and appreciate the terrain over which the Battle of Passchendaele was fought.

There are now 11,956 Commonwealth servicemen of the First World War buried or commemorated here. Of these, 8,369 burials are unidentified but there are special memorials to more than 80 casualties known or thought to be buried among them.

Tyne Cot Memorial forms the north-eastern boundary of Tyne Cot Cemetery and commemorates nearly 35,000 servicemen from the United Kingdom and New Zealand who died in the Ypres Salient after 16 August 1917 and whose graves are not known.

There is a visitor centre with a small display about the Cemetery.

Visit if You Can

Memorial Museum Passchendaele 1917
Ieperstraat 7A
Zonnebeke
www.passchendaele.be
Open daily (not 16 December–31 January)
Admission charge

A relatively new museum in an old chateau rebuilt in the 1920s, it is an easy walk from Tyne Cot. The highlight here is probably an immersive trench experience, complete with corrugated iron walkways, dugouts, dim lights and a soundtrack full of exploding shells and whistling bullets. There is also a large-scale model showing how the Battle of Passchendaele was fought on the ground, and which explains the tactics employed by both sides.

Sanctuary Wood Museum (Hill 62)
Canadalaan 26
Zillebeke (off the N8 to Ghelevult)
Open daily
Admission charge

Behind this cafe, with its core of regular drinkers, is one of the few remaining examples of trenches surviving in Flanders. This is the reason why most people visit the Museum. There is much more besides, all rather jumbled up and minimally labelled. Don't forget to look through the 'What the Butler Saw' Machines (Stereoscopes) to see some fairly graphic 3D images of the war. If you like everything labelled and rather sanitised then you won't like this Museum, but I think in its curious way it does rather effectively bring home the horrors of the war.

There are two other private museums in Zilllebeke displaying artefacts found on the battlefields or collected by their owners: Menin Road Museum found inside the Café Canada at Menseweg 470 (closed Tuesdays and Thursdays), and the Hooge Crater Museum, Menseweg 467 (closed Mondays).

Essex Farm Cemetery
Diksmudeweg
Boezinge
www.cwgc.org
Open daily
Admission free

This is perhaps the most visited cemetery in the Salient after Tyne Cot.

The land south of Essex Farm was used as a dressing station cemetery from April 1915 to August 1917. Because it was so close to the front, burials were made without definite plan and some of the divisions which occupied this sector may be traced in almost every part of the cemetery.

There are 1,200 men buried here including that of Rifleman Valentine John Strudwick, who was only 15 at the time of his death.

It was in Essex Farm Cemetery that Lieutenant-Colonel John McCrae of the Canadian Army Medical Corps wrote the poem 'In Flanders Fields' in May 1915.

Look out also for the concrete bunkers that once housed the dressing station. They have been restored and can be visited.

In Bargiestraaat, which is an industrial estate nearby, a small segment of trench – known as the Yorkshire Trench – was excavated in 1997 by volunteer archaeologists.

Interesting Places

St George's Memorial Church
Elverdingsestrrat 1
Ieper
Open daily
Admission free

Slightly away from central Ypres, this church was built between the wars to service the religious needs of the large British community who settled in the town after the end of the war mainly to work within the cemeteries. The community has now almost entirely been absorbed into the local population, but the Church remains immaculately kept with many memorials to men and regiments who fought in the Salient. It is a good place to reflect on what you have seen after a day out on the battlefields.

Ramparts War Museum
Rijelsestraat 3
Ieper
http://rampartswarmuseumypres.com/index.html

Open every day except Wednesdays and Thursdays
Admission charge

This is a small private museum that was originally part of a bar.
Indeed, you still walk through the bar to enter the Museum. There
is a fine collection of items retrieved from the battlefields as well
as some manikins recreating scenes in the trenches. Perhaps of
most interest is the location: it is thought this was where the
famous trench newspaper the *Wipers Times* was first published.
Writing in 1930, the editor Lieutenant-Colonel F. J. Roberts
remembered that: 'We had a piano – loot from a neighbouring
cellar where it had been propping up the remains of a house – a
gramophone, a printing-press and a lot of subalterns [junior
officers].' It is also close to the Ramparts Cemetery.

De Cellen
Guido Gezellestraat
Poperinge
Open Daily
Admission Free

In this courtyard behind the Town Hall (Stadhuis) a number of
British deserters were 'Shot at Dawn'. The two cells in which the
soldiers spent their last nights are preserved and you can still see
the graffiti they scribbled on the walls.

Lijssenthoek Military Cemetery
Boescheppeweg 35A
Poperinge
www.cwgc.org
Open daily
Admission free

This cemetery is second only to Tyne Cot in size. Close to the front, but out of the extreme range of most German field artillery, Lijssenthoek was a natural place to establish Casualty Clearing Stations. The Cemetery was first used by the French 15th Hôpital D'Evacuation and in June 1915 it began to be used by CCSs of the Commonwealth forces.

The Cemetery contains 9,901 Commonwealth burials of the First World War, 24 being unidentified. There are 883 war graves of other nationalities, mostly French and German, but there is also a small number of graves of Chinese labourers who came from China in the closing months of the war.

Bayernwald
Voormezelstraat
Wijtshate
Open daily
Admission charge (buy tickets from the Wijtshate tourist office)

A surviving stretch of carefully restored German trenches, of which about 10 per cent is open to the public. Nearby is the attractive 'Pool of Peace', or the Spanbroekmolen Mine Crater, the site of one of the nineteen mines exploded on 7 June 1917 as part of the Battle of Messines.

Irish Peace Park
Armentiersesteenweg
Mesen
Open daily
Admission free

A memorial to the men from Ireland, both north and south, who died during the First World War. The design is based on a traditional Irish watchtower. Nearby is the Messines Ridge Cemetery with the New Zealand Memorial to the Missing with over 800 names inscribed on the walls.

Further Reading

You can find out more about the travel, hotels and so on through the excellent Visit Flanders website at www.visitflanders.co.uk. TripAdvisor (www.tripadvisor.co.uk) will provide candid assessments of attractions, hotels and so on. If you are planning a trip it is also well worth visiting the World War One Battlefields website, which has lots of background information, at www.ww1battlefields.co.uk/flanders.html. Also helpful are the various essays on Tom Morgan's Hellfire Corner website at www.hellfirecorner.co.uk, which recount individual experiences of visiting 'France and Flanders'.

There are a number of guidebooks available to help you find your way around. The best one is undoubtedly Major and Mrs Holt's *Pocket Battlefield Guide to Ypres and Passchendaele* (Pen & Sword, 2012). An unusual work, written with walkers and cyclists in mind (although it is also ideal for motorists), is Jon Cooksey and Jerry Murland's *Battle Lines: Ypres Nieuwpoort to Ploegsteert* (Pen & Sword, 2013), which offers routes to twenty-five key areas of interest. Other useful guides are Wayne Evans and Staf Schoesters's *Silent Cities of Flanders Fields: The WWI Cemeteries of Ypres Salient and West Flanders* (Lanoo, 2013), and Ted Smith and Tony Spagnoly's *A Walk around Plugsteert* (Pen & Sword, 1997).

For the Western Front as a whole Rose Coombe's *Before Endeavours Fade* (After the Battle, 2006) is highly recommended. A more basic introduction is Bradt's *World War I Battlefields: A Travel Guide to the Western Front* (Bradt, 2014). Unfortunately, it is much harder to buy a decent large-scale map of the area, although the best are produced by NGI (www.ngi.be), which also publishes a thematic map, '1914–1918 the Great War from Liege to the Yser and the Somme'. However, the map of the Western Front sold by tourist offices and many souvenir shops is rather poor.

GLOSSARY OF PLACE NAMES

Flanders was (and remains) a Flemish-speaking area. However, foreigners, including the British Army's High Command, generally preferred to use the French names of towns.

To add to the linguistic confusion, the British Army either mangled local names or, more often, added a whole raft of new names to the landscape. Most farms, for example, were unnamed or referred to by the name of their owner. The British gave them all names. Mouse Trap Farm, which saw heavy fighting in April and May 1915, was originally just referred to as a 'Chateau' on Belgian maps. It was originally called Shell Trap Farm, but was renamed with something more positive on Corps orders.

In this book I have used place names as they were used at the time, as this is generally easier for the historian: so Ieper appears as Ypres.

As a result of tensions between the Flemish and Walloon populations in Belgium all place names in Flanders are now in Flemish, so you will need to know that Ypres is shown as Ieper on roadmaps and road signs.

Here is a table showing the key towns in Flemish, French and English.

Dutch	French	English	German
Ieper	Ypres	Wipers	Ypern
Geluvard		Ghelevelt	
Passendale		Passchendaele	
Poperinge	Poperinghe	Pops	
Ploegsteert		Plug Street	

Menen	Menin	Menin	
Roeselare	Roulers		
Mesen	Messines		
Kortrijk	Courtrai		
Nieuwpoort	Nieuport		
Loker	Locre		
Wijtscate		Whitesheet	
Geluveld	Gheluvelt		

A full list will be found in any decent guide to the battlefields of the area.

TIMELINE

There were a number of major battles in the Ypres Salient:

- First Battle of Ypres (October–November 1914);
- Second Battle of Ypres (April–May 1915);
- Third Battle of Ypres (better known as the Battle of Passchendaele) (July–November 1917);
- Fourth Battle of Ypres (April 1918);
- The Final Breakout (sometimes called the Fifth Battle of Ypres) (September–October 1918).

Within these battles the British Battles Nomenclature Committee later identified lesser actions, many of which are given below. Where appropriate I have included details of relevant publications, which will be of use if you want to find out more. Unless indicated the publisher is Pen & Sword.

The First Battle of Ypres, 12 October–22 November 1914

Between 27 and 29 October 1914 the Belgian Army halted the German attacks by flooding the Yser plain, while to the south the British and French fought with great determination to prevent a German breakthrough at Ypres. When the battle was over, the Germans held a ring of high ground overlooking the city. Both armies dug in and the famous Ypres Salient was born.

General Books
Beckett, Ian F. C., *Ypres: the First Battle*, Routledge, 2006
Fowler, William, *Battle Story: Ypres*, The History Press, 2011

Gliddon, Gerald, *VCs of the First World War: 1914,* The History Press, 2011

Lomas, David, *First Ypres 1914: the Graveyard of the Old Contemptibles*, Osprey, 1998

Sheldon, Jack, *The German Army at Ypres 1914,* 2010

Battle of Messines, 12 October–2 November
Cave, Nigel and Jack Sheldon, *Ypres 1914: Messines,* 2014

Battle of Armentières, 13 October–2nd November

Battle of Ypres, 19 October–22 November 1914
Cave, Nigel, *Ypres 1914: The Menin Road,* 2014

Battle of Langemark, 21–4 October
Cave, Nigel and Jack Sheldon, *Ypres 1914: Langemarck,* 2014

Battle of Gheluvelt, 29 October–31 October

Battle of Nonnenboschen, 11th November

The Second Battle of Ypres, 22 April–25 May 1915

In the spring of 1915 the Germans made a new attempt to break through Ypres, starting by capturing Hill 60. On 22 April 1915 they used chlorine gas for the first time in modern warfare. The result was death, panic and total surprise and the Allies were forced to withdraw several miles – but there was no breakthrough. The following September the Germans were taken by surprise when the British used gas in their attack at Loos.

General Books
Batchelor, Peter and John Matson, *VCs of the First World War: the Western Front, 1915,* The History Press, 2011

Cooksey, John, *Flanders, 1915,* 2005
Dixon, John, *Magnificent but Not War,* 2009
Lee, John, *The Gas Attack,* 2009

Battle of Gravenstafel, 22–3 April

Battle of St Julien, 24 April–4 May
Keach, Graham, *St Julien,* 2001

Battle of Frezenberg, 8–13 May

Battle of Bellewearde, 24–5 May
McEntee-Taylor, Carole, *The Battle of Bellewaarde, June 1915,* 2014
www.bellewaarde1915.co.uk

The Third Battle of Ypres, 31 July–10 November 1917

On 7 June, during the mine battle at Messines, a total of nineteen mines were detonated under the German lines, creating deafening explosions that could be heard as far away as London.

The ensuing Battle of Passchendaele was devastating for the Allied front. The mere mention of the word Passchendaele conjures up images of the futility of war, bungling generalship and mud and it continues to dominate public perceptions of the First World War to this day. Over 4 months 400,000 British soldiers were either killed, wounded or went missing and during the battle they gained just 5 miles of ground. The Germans had built almost impregnable concrete bunkers, defended with machine guns.

In his war memoirs, David Lloyd George, the British Prime Minister, devoted 27 pages to the successful Hundred Days Offensive of 1918. He devoted over 100 pages to Third Ypres. This is a campaign that has been fought, and continues to be fought, through the medium of print.

General Books

Barton, Peter, *Passchendaele: Unseen Panoramas of the Third Battle of Ypres*, 2007

Cave, Nigel, *Ypres: Passchendaele*, 1997

Hart, Peter and Nigel Steel, *Passchendaele*, 2001

Liddle, Peter, *Passchendaele in Perspective*, 2013

Macdonald, Andrew, *Passchendaele: Anatomy of a Tragedy*, HarperCollins, 2014

Macdonald, Lyn, *They Called it Passchendaele*, Penguin, 1993

Marix Evans, Martin, *Passchendaele: the Hollow Victory*, 2005

Sheldon, Jack, *The German Army at Passchendaele*, 2014

Snelling, Stephen, *Victoria Cross Winners at Passchendaele*, The History Press, 2014

Warner, Philip, *Passchendaele*, 1997

Battle of Messines, 7–14 June

Cave, Nigel, *Hill 60*, 1997

Gliddon, Gerald, *VCS of the First World War: Arras and Messines*, The History Press, 2012

Oldham, Peter, *Messines Ridge*, 1997

Passingham, Ian, *Pillars of Fire*, The History Press, 2012

Battle of Pilkem Ridge, 31 July–2 August

Battle of Langemark, 16–18 August

Battle of Menin Road, 20–5 September

Battle of Polygon Wood, 26 September–3 October

Cave, Nigel, *Polygon Wood*, 1998

Battle of Broodseinde, 4 October

Smith, Ted and Tony Spagnoly, *Anatomy of a Raid*, 1997

Battle of Poelkapelle, 9 October

First Battle of Passchendaele, 12 October

Second Battle of Passchendaele, 26 October–10 November

The Fourth Battle of Ypres, 9–29 April 1918

In the spring of 1918 the German forces were strengthened by the arrival of fresh divisions from the Eastern Front, where the October Revolution of 1917 had led to Russia's withdrawal from the war. During the Battle of Merkem on 17 April 1918 the Belgian Army fought and withstood a relentless attack by the Germans which resulted in the enemy being forced back to their original positions by nightfall. However, in the Battle of Mount Kemmel the French were particularly hard-pressed and on 25 April this strategically important hill was lost to the Germans and Ypres was almost captured. Civilians and non-essential personnel from Poperinge and areas to the rear were ordered to leave the Salient in case of a German breakthrough.

Battle of Lys, 9–29 April
Baker, Chris, *The Battle for Flanders: German Defeat on the Lys, 1918,* 2011
Tomaselli, Phil, *The Battle of the Lys, 1918,* 2011

Battle of Estaires, 9–11 April

Second Battle of Messines, 10–11 April

Battle of Hazebrouck, 12–15 April

Battle of Bailleul, 13–15 April

First Battle of Kemmel, 17–19 April

Battle of Bethune, 18 April

Second Battle of Kemmel, 25–6 April

Battle of Scherpenberg, 29 April

The Final Breakout, 28 September–19 October 1918

By now German reserves had been exhausted and the Americans were starting to arrive on the Western Front in huge numbers. Meanwhile, the German home front began to disintegrate, and from 28 September until the Armistice on 11 November, a series of Allied offensives pushed the Germans back to the Scheldt River. The beginning of the Breakout was the Battle of Houthulst Forest on 28 September when the Belgian Army attacked the fortress in Houthulst Forest. Almost every Belgian unit was involved in the attack, which was supported by the British Second Army and a number of French divisions, and by the end of the first day the Belgians had succeeded in capturing the German lines along a front 11 miles wide and 4 miles deep. The next few weeks saw the British, Belgians, French and Americans push the Germans further and further back towards the Rhine.

General Books
Pitt, Barrie, *1918: The Last Act*, 2013

Fifth Battle of Ypres, 28 September–2 October

Battle of Courtrai, 14–19 October

The breakdown of battles and actions is given in more detail in T. A. James, *A Record of the Battles and Engagements of the British*

Armies in France and Flanders (originally published in 1924, but long out of print), which is helpful and available online at http://tinyurl.com/kqzwpg. It is also discussed in Beatrix Brice, *The Battle Book of Ypres* (1928, repr. Pen & Sword, 2014).

BIBLIOGRAPHY

Books

There must be several thousand books about the Western Front, and in particular the Ypres Salient and the men who fought there. The first came out within months of the outbreak of war. And no doubt many more will be published to coincide with the centenary. As well as editions in hardback or paperback, most of the titles described below are also available as e-books, ideal for you take with you to the battlefields. As well as the general bibliography, the Timeline includes lists of books for specific battles and actions.

Pen & Sword, the publishers of this book, have published a number of titles on the battles around Ypres. They are all listed by battle in the Timeline. You may find them in museum bookshops and at the excellent bookshop at TNA, but in general it is best to order them online at www.pen-and-sword.co.uk. And, of course, your local bookshop should be able to obtain them for you.

The British Army

Holmes, Richard, *Tommy: the British Soldier on the Western Front*, Harper, 2011

Rawson, Andrew, *The British Army, 1914–1918,* The History Press, 2014

Robertshaw, Andrew, *24 Hour Trench: A Day in the Life of Tommy*, The History Press, 2012

Shipton, Elizabeth, *Female Tommies*, The History Press, 2014

Memoirs and Diaries

This is a small selection of books currently in print.

Glogowski, Phillippe, *Ypres Memories*, T. J. Editions, 2014, a graphic novel

Gordon, Huntley, *The Unreturning Army*, Doubleday, 2013

Priddey, Doreen, *A Tommy at Ypres*, Amberley, 2013

Rowbotham, Mark, *Mud, Blood and Bullets*, The History Press, 2014

Roynon, Gavin, *Ypres Diary, 1914–1915: The Memoirs of Sir Morgan Crofton*, The History Press, 2013

General Histories of the War

There are numerous general histories of the war that are worth looking at if you want to put Ypres into context.

Addington, Scott, *First World War 100*, The History Press, 2014

Banks, Arthur, *A Military Atlas of the First World War*, 1975, repr. Pen & Sword, 2014

Connarty, Ian et al., *At The Going Down of the Sun*, Lannoo, 2001

Hart, Peter, *The Great War 1914–18*, Profile, 2014

Holmes, Richard, *The Western Front*, BBC, 2008

Palmer, Ian, *The Salient: Ypres 1914–1918*, Constable, 2007

Stevenson, David, *1914–1918: the History of the First World War*, Penguin, 2012

Strachan, Hew, *The First World War*, Simon & Shuster, 2014

Travers, Tim, *The Killing Ground*, Pen & Sword, 2009

Websites

There are a number of websites that can help your research, most of which are listed in the appropriate place in the text of this book. However, Wikipedia has some excellent pages on the Western Front and the battles that were fought there. For all aspects of the British Army and its organisation you need to use Chris Baker's superb Long, Long Trail site at www.1914-1918.net.

The Western Front Association's website at www.westernfront association.com has masses of information about all aspects of the war, and contributions from members and non-members alike are welcomed.

Also of interest are the Great War (www.greatwar.co.uk) and Hellfire Corner (www.hellfirecorner.co.uk) websites, although here the emphasis is more on the battles and battlefield tourism.

The WW1 Photos website at www.ww1photos.com contains many photographs of individual officers and soldiers with the occasional transcript from books and indexes. Extracts from a number of personal diaries of the period can be found at www.war-diary.com.

INDEX